What some are saying. . .

Every once in a while, a book comes along that touches my heart in a way that echoes my thoughts and feelings. If you only read one devotional this year, make it *Making Eye Contact with God* and find something new in your relationship with the Lord you never knew was missing.
--Wanda Dyson, critically acclaimed suspense author of the *Shefford Case Files.*

What greater praise can I give for a book than my gratitude? *Making Eye Contact with God* helped me do just that—raise my eyes to my Lord— in a difficult time. Ms. Gillespie's devotional blessed me in a wonderful way, and I know this book will bless so many more.
--Kathryn Mackel, author of *The Hidden*

In *Making Eye Contact with God*, Terri Gillespie escorts us into the secret place where we can regularly meet with Abba, our heavenly Father. Whether you are Jewish or Gentile, this book will help you explore the most secret and vulnerable places of your heart, while you gaze into the loving eyes of the Messiah.
--Dr. Angela Hunt, Christy-Award winning author of *The Face, Magdalene* and *The Shadow Women*

Brew a cup of tea and steal away with this treasure trove brimming with godly wisdom! These heartfelt anecdotes gleaned from life's journey of faith coupled with applicable Scriptures are sure to powerfully impact your world! Written with delightful humor and tenderness, each devotional is refreshingly relevant and challenging to anyone seeking to know Messiah more intimately.
--Kathy Shooster, Messianic Songwriter/Recording Artist

Thank you for the inspiration *Making Eye Contact with God* will bring to the women into whose blessed hands it falls. I know from personal experience.
--Debra Chernoff, Rebbitzen, Congregation Beth Yeshua/Songwriter/speaker

Making Eye Contact with God is an extremely reflective, inspiring and motivating message, one women of all ages will relate to. While reading, I often had to pause to take in what was being downloaded into my spirit. I'm so glad that a devotional like this finally exists! Terri's transparency woos you to become a model of transparency and authenticity in your own life. As she wrote, "The greatest form of intimacy is to look the Lord 'in the eye' with the confidence of someone who knows who they are in the Messiah."
--Sharon Chernoff Wilbur, Songwriter/Recording artist

MAKING
Eye Contact
WITH
GOD

MAKING
Eye Contact
WITH
GOD

~ *A Weekly Devotional for Women* ~

TERRI GILLESPIE

Lederer Books
A division of
Messianic Jewish Publishers
Clarksville, Maryland

Unless otherwise noted, scripture quotations are taken from:

Complete Jewish Bible © 1998 by David H. Stern,
Published by Messianic Jewish Publishers

Cover Design by
Josh Huhn, Design Point, Inc.
Interior design and page layout by
Transcontinental Transmédia,
Marie-Ève Poirier

12 11 10 9 8   5 4 3 2 1

ISBN: 978-1-880226-51-3

Library of Congress Control Number: 2008927264
Printed in Canada

Lederer Books
A division of
Messianic Jewish Publishers
6120 Day Long Lane
Clarksville, MD 21029

Distributed by
Messianic Jewish Resources International
Order Line: (800) 410-7367
E-mail: lederer@messianicjewish.net
Website: www.messianicjewish.net

This book is dedicated to the women
God has graciously placed in my life
to open my eyes.

Contents

Introduction

It Began With a Sparrow

The eyes are the windows of the soul.

I received a vivid revelation of this phrase when I heard what sounded like a bird riot outside my house.

Somehow a sparrow had trapped itself between the storm window and regular window. He frantically threw his tiny body against the glass to escape. His bird buddies fluttered around the window until they spotted me at which point they quickly abandoned their friend.

I unlocked the sash and lifted it a few inches. The sparrow became so agitated that I was afraid the little guy would have a heart attack. What if he flew into the house? I'd have a bigger problem on my hands.

How could I safely remove him? I began speaking in soothing tones as I attempted to guide him into my hand. It wasn't working. My words of comfort switched to prayers.

Impulsively, I grabbed the sparrow by the tail feathers. With my other hand, I formed a cell for the frightened captive. He reacted more violently than I expected. I could barely hold him with both hands. How was I going to open the doors and release him?

I continued to alternately speak to him and pray.

Then, we made eye contact.

His shiny bead-like eyes connected with mine. Immediately, his struggle ceased. I was able to remove one hand. He sat quietly in my palm as I opened the doors. Seconds later, he was free, and I was left in wonder.

For months afterward, every time I saw a sparrow, I replayed the event in my head. As much as I hated to admit it, the incident seemed like a graphic picture of my relationship with God.

How many times had he reached out to rescue me, but I flew away in fear or confusion? How often was he forced to grab me by the tail feathers to prevent me from getting into more trouble? How many times had he held me in his hand only to have me fight him because I thought I was trapped?

How much easier would it have been if I had turned my eyes toward the Lord—to make eye contact with him?

I also thought about the fact that this little bird lived its life fulfilling the purpose God had created for it. It had no identity crises about what it should be; the sparrow simply was. Was that why it was so easy for the little guy to trust me—the bird connected with his Creator's Spirit living in me?

As I meditated further, I wondered how much of my life was fulfilling God's purposes. Is that why I struggled to maintain eye contact with God? Were there other issues that kept me from an intimate relationship with him?

A Messianic and Christian Women's Devotional

On Rosh HaShanah (the Jewish New Year) in 1995, God called my husband, Bob, and me to the Messianic Jewish movement. Although my husband later learned he had a Jewish background, he wasn't raised Jewish.

Both of us had been believers since the 1970s, but our lives changed as we became members a Messianic Synagogue in Philadelphia. Learning the Jewish roots of the faith in this environment was life altering.

For me as a non-Jewish believer in the Jewish Messiah, my place is now forever linked with the Jewish People, and my heart longs for the restoration of Israel. Like Ruth in the Bible, I became part of the Jewish community. This book is my gift to my family— my family by adoption.

For my Christian sisters, blood of my blood, this book is for you, too. As a reminder, dear sisters, the true unity between Jew and Gentile began with women, Ruth and Naomi. What seemed impossible was possible when God used the love these women had for each other.

Making Eye Contact with God contains many stories based on real women—both Jewish and non-Jewish women. I challenge you to tell the difference. Obviously, we all share the fundamental desire for a more intimate relationship with the Lord.

Having attended many women's retreats, I have discovered there's a wonderful culture that develops when women are away from life's distractions. They can be open, vulnerable, and sassy. During fellowship and worship, we can go without makeup, wear comfortable clothing, and remove our shoes. Those who don't dance can stumble through the hora, and those who can't sing praise the Lord off-key as loud as they want (I fall into both categories).

For a few days, we use feminine-speak and don't worry that someone won't understand. We explore the possibilities of what God might be saying to us personally, as women. It's the mystical combination of spending time away from our responsibilities with women who love one another in a place where our God shows up.

That's the safe, fun, and spiritual setting I want for both Messianic and Christian women in Making Eye Contact with God.

How to Use the Making Eye Contact with God Devotional

This weekly devotional is broken into two parts: The Eyes That Keep Us from Seeing God and The Eyes God Longs for Us to Have. Readers can work the devotions in sequence or skip around for themes relevant to their situation.

Each devotional contains a scriptural reference followed by a humorous or touching story, allegory, or biblical anecdote that illustrates other women's practical applications to the theme. After a prayer for the week, there is a section of thoughtful questions for meditation and spiritual exercises, useful in studies for an individual and/or group.

There are handy endnotes and Hebrew and Yiddish translations for those unfamiliar with certain terms.

My prayer for you, dear sisters, is that you will be challenged, motivated, surprised, and blessed by this book. I have it on good authority that God is most anxious to meet with you within these pages. He longs to make eye contact with you and reveal his and your heart. See you there!

In Yeshua's love,
Terri Gillespie
May 2008

Part One
The Eyes That Keep Us From Seeing God

*T*he Secret Place. A few years ago, if you had asked me what the Secret Place was and how to get there, I'd have checked my watch and made some excuse about being late for an appointment.

Why? Because I didn't have a clue what it was or where I could find it, and I was too embarrassed to ask anyone. There were plenty of occasions when I connected deeply with the Lord and wondered if I was in the neighborhood of the Secret Place, but I knew if I wanted to, I couldn't find my way back on my own.

Then, my rabbi's wife asked me to speak at one of our women's retreats and guess what the theme was?

As I meditated and prayed in preparation for my message, I uncovered the mystery: the Secret Place was where God and I made contact—emotionally, spiritually, and in some ways, physically.

Why did I have so much trouble seeing something so simple? I had lost my way because there were issues in my life that had hidden the precious path to my beloved. The windows to my soul were clouded, cluttered, and unable to focus.

The next five chapters explore some of the eye conditions— downcast, closed, tired, hardened, and unhealthy eyes—that prevent us from making eye contact with the Lord. If we are willing to battle what the enemy and our own flesh have done to blind us, the Lord will battle alongside us. As someone said, "You can't have a victory without a battle."

Take a deep breath and get ready to taste and see the goodness of the Lord.

Chapter One

Downcast Eyes

*H*ave you ever been introduced to someone who wouldn't make eye contact with you because his or her eyes were downcast? In our Western culture, an adult with downcast eyes generally conveys a negative impression. It's difficult to connect with someone who won't look at us.

Downcast eyes can signal problems with insecurity, anxiety, and guilt. They can also indicate more serious issues such as self-righteousness and unforgiveness.

Week One ~ Insecure Eyes

Are You a Porch Swing or a Tractor?

> *"For indeed the body is not one part but many . . . if the ear says, 'I'm not an eye, so I'm not part of the body,' that doesn't make it stop being part of the body."*
> 1 Corinthians 12:14,16

The old insecurities rolled in like a dark cloud.

A conversation with my friend about intimacy with the Lord and Secret Places brought back how awkward and clumsy I had always felt in life. In the hallowed Secret Place, surely God must favor someone like my friend—gorgeous, slender, and soft-spoken with a voice that would move angels. I imagined elegant women like her waiting for the Lord in their bucolic Secret Place, swinging on porch swings with fragrant flowers everywhere. Beautiful praises pour from their lips.

The Lord appears in the distance and opens his arms. The stunning women skip and twirl gracefully into his loving embrace. Together, they walk into the sunset holding hands; butterflies dance about their heads, and birds chirp sweetly.

Then, I imagined me in my Secret Place. Vrroom! Vrroom! I wait on a tractor belching smoke and fumes. Off in the distance, I see the Lord. He opens his arms. My foot presses the accelerator. I'm bouncing over mounds of dirt, whistling (because I can't sing), and pulling a trailer full of yesterday's and today's responsibilities to show the Lord how much I do for him. Although he smiles, he's also coughing and waving away exhaust fumes. I pause, cup a hand to my ear, and listen as God yells his message of love to me above the noise.

The elegant worshippers must have God's favor, right? My clumsiness must be a barrier to true intimacy with the Lord. That's what I've told myself. I can't raise my eyes toward him because I'm ashamed that my very nature disrupts the quiet and tranquility of the Secret Place.

Insecurities keep us from making eye contact with the Lover of our soul. The truth is each of us is capable of pleasing and loving God in ways no one else can. He formed us for that purpose—to praise him. And his Word tells us that he loves all types of praise and worship (Ps. 148).

Do you love the quiet type of praise and adoration in the morning? God does, too.

Or maybe you love to talk out loud to him as you take an evening stroll and enjoy his creation. He loves that, too.

Perhaps you take pleasure in worshipping him in dance, even if you are too afraid to participate in your congregation. Know that he also takes pleasure in this.

The greatest form of intimacy is to look the Lord "in the eye" with the confidence of someone who knows his or her identity in the Messiah. Think about this the next time you feel distracted with thoughts of how you aren't like someone else.

Now, I know he looks forward to me on my tractor. And I try to remember that my trailer of good deeds and responsibilities isn't what makes me attractive to the Lord. He simply wants—me. I still struggle with the insecurities, but I'm not as shy about trying new ways of worshipping and praising the Lord—I even climb off my tractor from time to time.

This week, allow the Lord to introduce you to you. Permit him to reveal those insecurities that keep your eyes downcast. Explore who you are in the Secret Place—with the One who created you.

Okay, Lord, you made me.

Help me to be the best tractor—or porch swing—I can be. This week, expose the areas of insecurity keeping me from making eye contact with you. And Lord, I also want to explore the unique ways you created me to praise and worship you.

I commit this week to learn how to overcome my insecurities and take joy in who you created me to be—even if it's a little scary and I discover that I'm even more unique than I thought. In Yeshua's Name. Amen.

Let's take it to the Secret Place:

Are there insecurities that keep me from freely worshipping the Lord in my Secret Place? In the congregation? What are they?

_____

_____

_____

_____

How do insecurities manifest themselves at these times? What do I hear that is contrary to God's Word?

_____

_____

_____

What are my unique qualities? How can I praise God through them?

_____

_____

_____

End of Week One:

What did I learn about my insecurities? What did I learn about my uniqueness? How did God speak to me in my Secret Place? Has our relationship improved? In what ways?

_____

_____

_____

Week Two ~ Anxious Eyes

What's the Password?

> "... Including you, who have been called by Yeshua the Messiah. To: All those in Rome whom God loves, who have been called, who have been set apart for him ..."
>
> Romans 1:6,7a

Remember those childhood years of tree houses, forts, and secret clubs where only those invited were given the secret password? The more obscure the word, the better to keep out the possible interlopers—especially little brothers or sisters—or perhaps someone who wasn't cool enough to be in the club.

Talya was one of those uncool kids. She was always the one on the outside, trying her best to discover that elusive password. She tried to create her own clubs, but no one wanted to join. Her childhood was spent frantically trying to figure out the secret code to fitting in.

As an adult, Talya tried to mold herself into women she felt were successful. Although having role models and mentors are valuable, Talya sought the false perfection of women in movies, on television, or in magazines. Even when she had been able to fashion herself into a persona, it was temporary because she exhausted herself trying to keep up the imitation.

Talya had no idea who she was or where she could fit in because she had never taken the time to get to know the person God had created her to be. She always felt anxious and unsure of herself. Would she ever know her true self and where she belonged?

In your Secret Place with the Lord, do you feel like that little kid struggling for the right password to get into the club? Or, like Talya, who has lost her identity in her efforts to be someone else?

Sometimes when we try to connect with God, we can feel like we are forever searching for the right "password" to gain acceptance into his presence. There *must* be a correct sequence of phrases that will open the gates of blessings or a sequence of effort that ensures God's favor.

But this is not where God wants us to be. We're already in the club.

The password to this exclusive club is *Yeshua*—his atonement through his death and resurrection is our membership.

We belong.

And the awesome thing is God wants as many people in the club as possible. He wants us to tell that password—Yeshua—to as many people as we can. God wants us to enjoy being in that club and explore fresh, new ways to get to know him and worship him.

On Talya's forty-fourth birthday, she finally understood she was already in the most exclusive and supreme club in the world—God's family. Talya has spent the last ten years getting to know herself and the Lord in the Secret Place. Imagine her surprise when she learned that younger women now sought her to mentor *them*!

This week, let's ask the Lord to show us any areas where we might feel anxiety because we are trying to be someone we're not or where we are unsure of his acceptance. Then, ask him to open opportunities for us to share his password with those he brings into our lives.

Thank you, *Abba (Daddy)*, for including me in your club. I never have to feel like an outsider again. Show me areas of anxiety and concern that keep my eyes downcast.

As you raise my eyes toward your beautiful face, show me ways to let others, still on the outside, know that there is one place where they truly belong. In Yeshua's Name. Amen.

Let's take it to the Secret Place:

Are there any areas where I feel uncool and unaccepted by God? How does that manifest itself in my life?

_____

_____

Write out three passages about God's acceptance of me (*E.g., Matt. 10:29–31, John 3:16, Rom. 8:38, 39*).

_____

_____

_____

_____

_____

Do I know outsiders with whom I can share my password? Who are they?

_____

_____

_____

End of Week Two:

Did God open any opportunities to share the password with someone this week? If yes, what happened? Has this impacted my time with the Lord in the Secret Place? In what ways?

_____

_____

_____

_____

Week Three ~ Guilty Eyes

Come Out, Come Out, Wherever You Are

> "Pain [sorrow] handled in God's way produces a turning from sin to God which leads to salvation, and there is nothing to regret in that! But pain [sorrow] handled in the world's way produces only death."
>
> 2 Corinthians 7:10

When you were a child, where did you hide when you were in trouble? Where do you go today?

The people of Mara's congregation attributed her harried countenance and quick anger to tending to two lively toddlers, her frequent debilitating migraines, and the needs of a husband who traveled. She made excuses to her rabbi's wife and the women in her Bible study that she was too busy to go to meetings. Her concerned friends gave her encouragement and prayed for her, which only made Mara feel worse.

Mara felt guilty because she hid a secret that was growing from a squall to a Katrina-sized hurricane and was threatening to destroy her marriage and family.

Mara was addicted to her migraine pain medication.

The addiction was gradual. At first, she took the next dose a little sooner than the recommended four to six hours. The pain medication helped to take the edge off her frantic days, especially when her husband was out of town.

Gradually, she took the tablets when she had no headache and found she enjoyed the happy fog it produced. It was months before she acknowledged that she was taking small doses of the drug hourly.

At first, she was able to fool her doctor into additional prescriptions by claiming to drop bottles in the toilet or pills down the kitchen sink. Before long, the doctor called Mara and refused to write another prescription unless she sought counseling.

This meant she had to tell her already overworked husband who didn't need another problem to deal with. Mara's shame was so overpowering that she didn't know what to do or where to go.

Can we actually hide from God's sight like an errant child hides from her parents? Psalm 139 says that no matter where we are, he is there. Because he can see all of the way into our hearts, hiding from God is really about our not looking at him.

Guilt can keep our eyes downcast, as though we are hiding from God. As the passage above states, there are two types of guilt: the conviction by *Ruach HaKodesh* (the Holy Spirit), that leads to repentance and God's merciful forgiveness or the bondage of Satan that keeps us in hiding—distanced from God's love and freedom.

Mara went to her rabbi's wife and told her about the addiction. She prayed with Mara, which gave her the confidence to tell her husband. Although revealing her secret was difficult, Mara is glad her problem is out in the open and she no longer has to hide from others and God. Instead, she can rest in God's presence as the beloved forgiven daughter she is, which gives her strength as she overcomes this addiction.

Our heavenly Abba longs to make eye contact with us. What are the areas of guilt keeping us from him? Maybe it's our tendency toward hurtful gossip, or we've allowed a friendship with someone who isn't our husband to become too intimate, or we've been stealing from our employer.

Our Secret Place with him is a place of safety and the beginning of our healing and freedom. We don't need to hide from God; as we lift our eyes toward him in repentance, he will meet us with forgiveness. And by his grace and strength, he will help us work through any consequences.

El Nosey (Forgiving God), you have probed me, and you know me. You know when I sit and when I stand up, you discern my inclinations from afar, and you scrutinize my daily activities. You're so familiar with all of my ways that before I speak even a word, you know what I'm going to say (Ps. 139:1–4).

Examine me, God, and know my heart; test me, and know my thoughts. See if there is in me any hurtful way, and lead me along the eternal way (Ps. 139:23–24).

I can't hide from you, Abba. Really, I don't want to. You see everything. You are my only salvation and chance for a life of fullness. I love you. In Yeshua's Name. Amen.

Let's take it to the Secret Place:

Do I harbor guilt from past or current mistakes or sins? Have I taken these to the Lord? If yes, do I still feel guilt? If I haven't gone to the Lord yet, what is holding me back?

_____

_____

_____

_____

What usually is my initial response to guilt?

_____

_____

If there are areas of guilt, what do I need to do first? What is my next step?

_____

_____

End of Week Three:

What did I learn about how guilt can affect my relationship with the Lord? How did God speak to me in the Secret Place about guilt? Has our relationship improved? In what ways?

_____

_____

_____

_____

_____

_____

Week Four ~ Self-righteous Eyes

The Bigger Sin

> "... [Yeshua] spoke this parable to some who trusted in themselves that they were righteous, and despised others ... 'The Pharisee stood and prayed thus to himself, "God, I thank you that I am not like other men——extortioners, unjust, adulterers, or even as this tax collector," ... 'and the tax collector, standing far off, would not so much as raise his eyes to heaven, but beat his breast, saying, "God, be merciful to me a sinner!" I tell you the truth [the tax collector] went down to his house justified rather than the [Pharisee].'"
>
> *Luke 18:9-14 (NKJV)*

*N*aomi slammed the phone down. How much more could she take? She and her husband had tried to be the best parents that they could be. What seed had they sown in their eighteen-year-old son, Sam that produced such rebellion?

From the time Sam could speak, he expressed a desire to serve God. As their only child grew, his ideas for ministry were a little off the wall for their tastes—clearly not in line with his obvious God-given gifts. As his parents, they simply redirected their son down more fruitful paths.

However, over the last few years, Sam had begun to hang around a rougher crowd—to witness, he had said—and before Naomi and her husband knew it, their on-fire-for-the-Lord boy had turned into a dark, sullen young man whom they no longer recognized.

But that morning after no response to her knock on Sam's bedroom door, Naomi had entered to find an empty room, an empty closet, and a missing duffle bag. The daily squabbles had escalated to full-out rebellion.

"How could he?" she thought angrily. "How dare he leave without a word! And his first semester of college is just three weeks away."

By evening, Naomi's indignation had morphed into fear. What if her child was in the hands of molesters, bound, gagged, and doomed to the lost, like the children whose pictures were on milk cartons? What if he was in a ditch somewhere, bleeding and pleading hoarsely for her to find him?

Sam's phone call at midnight saying he was fine and not to worry was no relief. Especially with the added news that he and what's-her-name had moved in together. Then, he had asked if Naomi wanted to talk with the hussy?

That was when Naomi slammed down the phone, her stomach in knots. Her hurt and anger were so intense that she wanted to slap her poor husband when he had tried to comfort her.

Several weeks later during Naomi's devotion time, memories crept into her thoughts. Recollections of Sam coming to her with his far-out ideas of ministry interrupted her efforts to pray and study. She became uncomfortable remembering Sam's look of disappointment every time she redirected his efforts to more conventional pursuits. Her discomfort began feeling more like conviction. Was God telling her she had been wrong? That she had sinned against her son?

How could God be convicting her when Sam had sinned against her and God? Rebellion? Fornication? How could that compare with her mistaken opinion?

Naomi had every right to be angry with her son. She didn't need to ask him for forgiveness! Did she?

In Yeshua's parable, we have two men with downcast eyes. The tax collector had downcast eyes because he "humbled himself," but the Pharisee looked down on the tax collector and ignored his own sins (v. 14). It's a no-brainer to discern who was more pleasing to God. But why wouldn't the Pharisee know he was a sinner? Could it be the Pharisee felt no need to repent? Surely, the tax collector's sins were bigger than his were. Why would God convict the Pharisee when the tax collector had sinned against his own people and God?

Isaiah 64:6 says all of our righteous deeds are like menstrual rags. All those *mitzvot* (good deeds)—important to our sanctification though they may be—can't earn us one speck of righteousness. The worst sin is the sin for which we have not repented.

Eventually after several more months of God working on Naomi, she truly repented to the Lord for her own disobedience in not seeking his will for her son. But godly sorrow over discouraging Sam from God's calling nearly did her in.

This woman of God took that sin, sorrow, and guilt to the Lord in her Secret Place. Together, they worked through the ocean of emotions until she was able to also humble herself and reconcile with her son.

After her repentance, the Lord also helped Naomi work through the disappointment that her son didn't make a miraculous turnaround because of her courageous and obedient deed. He also helped her cope with the fact that when her son continues to sin, she is still accountable to the Lord for any sinful responses she might have. Naomi works to stop comparing her "smaller" sin to Sam's "larger" sin and instead just lets God continue to convict her and her beloved son.

This week, let's take a more careful look at those "little sins" that may be hidden by the "bigger sins" of others.

Avinu Sheba'shemayim (Our Father in Heaven), the lesson this week is especially important—and difficult. I don't want to disguise my sins or justify them in any way even if it's uncomfortable or it means I have to humble myself.

I'm sobered by Yeshua's parable. I don't want my honest efforts at godly behavior to be corrupted by comparing my abilities to others'. Whether voiced to others or in my thoughts, let me know if my eyes are looking down on them.

Right now, I repent of my past self-righteous acts. And, Lord, if I need to repent to others, please make that very clear. In Yeshua's Name. Amen.

Let's take it to the Secret Place:

Was there any particular incident or situation that came to mind as I read this devotion? If so, what?

_____

_____

_____

Do I often find myself comparing my performance to that of others? What pattern does that typically take?

_____

_____

_____

Have I ever had to humble myself like Naomi and reconcile with someone who I thought was a "bigger" sinner than me?

_____

_____

_____

End of Week Four:

Were there any lessons and actions from the Lord this week? What did I learn about my self-righteousness? How did God speak to me in the Secret Place? Has our relationship improved? In what ways?

_____

_____

_____

_____

Week Five~ Offended Eyes

Is It Worth It?

> *"ADONAI [Lord] said to Kayin [Cain], 'Why are you angry? Why so downcast? If you are doing what is good, shouldn't you hold your head high? And if you don't do what is good, sin is crouching at the door—it wants you . . . .'"*
>
> Genesiss 4:6,7

*E*sther tried to remember the last time that she had enjoyed coming to services. There was a time when she couldn't wait to see her congregational family and catch up on what God had done in their lives over the previous week. Esther even arrived a half-hour early so she could *schmooze* (socialize).

But lately, she arrived after praise and worship with her eyes focused on chairs and the floor and not the people. Esther sat in the back and skillfully avoided making eye contact with them.

Them—the growing number of people who had hurt, offended, or slighted her in some way. Esther's mind replayed the events and emotional wounds as the service continued. She saw people, like Annie who didn't invite her to her daughter's *bat mitzvah* or the rabbi who hadn't called her in two months to minister on the prayer team. She resented that these people were able to worship while she was hurting so deeply. Weren't they discerning enough to feel her pain? The thoughts of leaving her beloved congregation surfaced again. Why was this happening to her?

Offenses not only keep us from making eye contact with one another, but also with the Lord. In the Scripture portion above, Cain was upset that God didn't accept his offering. God's acceptance of his brother Abel's offering exacerbated the matter. The outcome was the first recorded murder. A brother murdered a brother. It's easy to assume as believers that we are exempt from such anger; however, there are disturbing statistics that indicate otherwise.

According to a recent survey of people who no longer attended a Bible-believing congregation, the second-most common category for leaving was disenchantment. Within that category, people felt leadership and/or congregants were hypocritical and judgmental or didn't support the people.[1] Another study indicates born-again believers are more likely to divorce than atheists or agnostics.[2]

Unfortunately, the people we love and respect the most are the ones who can hurt us the most profoundly. How do we handle the offense? Do we overlook it or get angry and confront the offending party?

Offenses and little squabbles can surface from time to time. Without realizing it, we can let them can grow into a full-blown debacle in our life and possibly the congregation as a whole.

Excluding seriously unhealthy relationships (violence or other abuses), we are instructed in God's Word to labor at reconciliation. Our goal is not to prove how right we are, but to reconcile.

Yeshua prayed for unity in John 17, that we would be one, as he and the Father are one. Why was unity so important to him? David Stern writes, "Healing of these splits is given an evangelistic purpose in Yeshua's prayer: may they be one in us so that the unsaved world may believe that you (God the Father) sent me (Yeshua)(emphasis mine)."[3]

So disunity impedes revival?
Perhaps there's a question we need to ask: Is this offense worth sacrificing someone's salvation?

Here's a little test I take from time to time. Sitting toward the back of the congregation, I take a few moments to look around. If I sense any resistance when making eye contact, I try to examine what emotions—hurt, anger, frustration, or guilt are churning inside me? If I can, I try to resolve it as quickly as possible.

If there are complex issues, then the safest place is taking it to the Secret Place, where the Lord will guide me as to how to resolve it. And, if need be, I will seek counsel from our leadership. The valuable outcome is the freedom to raise my eyes in the Secret Place and with my family.

This week, let's examine our downcast eyes for any offenses keeping us from unity at home, in our congregations, and at the office.

*L*ord, I get the seriousness of this. Yeshua prayed for unity because it impacts our relationship with him and world revival. This week, show me areas where my eyes are downcast in offense and anger. Father, walk me through the process by your grace, but ultimately, I know I just need to do it and not try to wiggle my way out of the discomfort. I need to repent, forgive, and work at reconciliation.

 I repent for this sin that wants to get the better of me. In Yeshua's Name. Amen.

Let's take it to the Secret Place:

Is there anyone in my congregation, at the office, or at home with whom I can no longer make eye contact?

_____

_____

_____

Can I identify the moment I lost contact with this person?

_____

_____

_____

Have I forgiven this person? Do I need to ask forgiveness of this person for my avoidance of them?

_____

_____

_____

End of Week Five:

What did I learn about how offenses change my relationship with the Lord? Was I able to reconnect with anyone I've avoided? Has this impacted my time with the Lord in the Secret Place? In what ways?

_____

_____

_____

_____

_____

Chapter Two

Closed Eyes

*W*ouldn't it be great if we could shut our eyes to the things that make us angry, disappointed, and afraid or to the disruptions of our lives?

Silly, right?

What if we are closing our eyes, spiritually? How does that affect our relationship with the Lord?

There are many reasons that we might close our eyes: anger, disappointment, fear, overwhelming circumstances, or unholy pursuits. Are you ready to check for closed eyes?

Week Six ~ Angry Eyes

Eyes Scrunched Shut

> "... [B]ecause the heart of this people has grown thick—with their ears they barely hear, and their eyes they have closed, for fear that they should see with their eyes, hear with their ears, understand with their heart, and do t'shuvah [turn, repent], so that I could heal them."
>
> Acts 28:27

There was no mistaking two-year-old Jessica was angry with her grandfather. She sat on the floor with a stiff pout that looked like she was carved from granite.

Grandfather was late—a whole hour—and in her young mind, that seemed like an eternity. She was fuming, and disregarded the attempts of her sisters to distract her.

Finally, Grandfather arrived. Little Jessica was not among his other grandchildren who joyfully greeted him. He searched until he found his youngest grandchild. He called to her but was answered with an irritated harrumph!

With a gentle laugh, the grandfather swooped up the fuming toddler, planted kisses on her chubby cheeks, and spoke lovingly to her. Despite the affection, Jessica scrunched shut her little eyes, lifted her chin, and ignored him. In her immature mind, she dismissed him.

We may smile at the tot's impudence, but have we ever been angry with or disappointed in God? As in God-the-Creator-of-the-Universe God?

All of us have experienced disappointments that can take the emotional slide into anger. Perhaps there's an expectation that has dragged on despite years of prayer? Or a hurt so deep we question God's sovereignty because he didn't protect us?

Perhaps some feel they could never be angry with God. He is perfect; therefore, we have no business being angry with him. This, of course, is true, and our goal is to work through crises with the grace of God. However, it's important for us to also know that God is not afraid of our anger. Like the grandfather, God's ultimate desire is reconciliation. He would prefer we were honest with him rather than hide our anger.

The prophet Jonah had certain expectations of God. He felt justified in his dislike of the people of Nineveh, who had persecuted Israel. Jonah went to great lengths to avoid taking God's message of salvation to them. Even after Jonah's harrowing nautical and gastric experiences, he resented the mission God asked of him.

Subsequent to dispatching God's message to the people of Nineveh, Jonah was angry. Not because his enemies had rejected God's message, but because the king and all of his people had accepted it. Jonah wanted God's wrath, not mercy or salvation, for Israel's persecutors.

Jonah cared more for a wilting plant than the people who were once his enemies.

Are we like Jonah? Are our perspectives distorted because things didn't turn out the way we had expected?

It's easy to justify our right to hold on to these emotions; however, in holding on to them even when we don't like the results of his will, we are closing our eyes to the truth that God is God and sovereign.

Just as Jessica's childish mind lacked the understanding of her grandfather's love and authority, perhaps we aren't seeing our Heavenly Father's hand in an area because we haven't realized our eyes are scrunched tight.

Our anger can close our eyes to a significant point God wants to communicate to us. We can't deal with issues to which we won't admit. Do we trust our Abba enough to open our eyes to a picture not of our choosing?

This week's Scripture discusses how our hearts can grow thick—calloused—and our eyes can close to the very healing God wants to perform in our lives.

Eventually, Jessica opened her eyes and realized that she loved her grandfather and he loved her. At the end of the day, we want the same.

God is holding us in his arms right now. He's lovingly speaking to our spirits. This week, let's open our eyes to the areas where we might be angry with or disappointed in God.

Oh, Abba, I want to open my eyes to anything keeping me from seeing you and your great love for me.

This week, please reveal, by your Ruach HaKodesh, any areas where I am disappointed in and angry about your will. Also, show me areas where I might be hiding these feelings.

In faith, I trust in your sovereignty, wisdom, and love. In Yeshua's Name. Amen.

Let's take it to the Secret Place:

Do I feel nervous about being angry with or disappointed in God? Why?

_____

_____

_____

_____

Has the Lord revealed areas where I might be hiding feelings of anger with or disappointment in him? If so, list those areas and begin releasing them to him.

_____

_____

_____

_____

_____

_____

End of Week Six:

What did I learn about how anger and disappointment can affect my relationship with the Lord? How did God speak to me in the Secret Place about my feelings? Has our relationship improved? In what ways?

_____

_____

_____

_____

Week Seven ~ Disappointed Eyes

Yet I Will Rejoice in the Lord. . .

> *"For even if the fig tree doesn't blossom, and no fruit is on the vines, even if the olive tree fails to produce, and the fields yield no food at all, even if the sheep vanish from the sheep pen, and there are no cows in the stalls; still, I will rejoice in ADONAI, I will take joy in the God of my salvation. Elohim ADONAI [the Lord God] is my strength! He makes me swift and sure-footed as a deer and enables me to stride over my high places.".*
>
> *Habakkuk 3:17-19*

Sarah replayed the devastating voicemail: "The test results are negative. Please call the doctor's office if you have any questions."

Tens of thousands of dollars, painful tests, hormone fluctuations that had sent her on a rollercoaster of emotions, and the fervent prayers of her synagogue—all for nothing, for the second time.

The disappointment was agonizing, but then, other thoughts plopped into the cauldron of emotions."Why God? Did I do something wrong? Not pray hard enough? Is there some sin I haven't repented of? Is it too late now; am I too old? Please Lord, not another round of pity—or judging from my friends and relatives. I'm a failure as a woman and wife."

Sarah sank lower into the depression when she remembered that tomorrow was her best friend's son's bar mitzvah. How could she sit and be happy for her friends while her heart and womb were empty? How could she watch as her friends lovingly placed the tallit (prayer shawl) over their handsome son's shoulders and spoke blessings over him as the boy became a young man?

Where do we go when the spiraling pain of disappointment knocks the very breath from our spirits? How can we look to God who has seemingly deprived us of our heart's desire? And not a frivolous want but a basic longing built into our nature by God himself?

There are no easy answers; truthfully, sometimes there are no answers at all. Some situations just are, and we have the mountainous job of working through the emotions, pain, and repercussions of these disappointments. But we can't do this alone.

Corrie ten Boom and her family heroically hid Jewish people from the Nazis in Holland. They were not rewarded with a Genesis 12:3 blessing; instead, the curse of the Nazis and suffering in a concentration camp were their rewards for helping God's people.

Corrie tormented herself searching for why, which became a raging need for justice in a filthy place of death and injustice. Her sister Betsie found peace in the acceptance of where she was and joy in worshiping the Lord amidst the filth and death.

However, anger and thoughts of revenge consumed Corrie. A hopeless cycle of disappointment, depression, and anger turned her into different person—a person who frightened her.

In her book, The Hiding Place, Corrie writes of the moment where she finally surrendered her disappointed expectations and accepted where she was. She chose to worship God and hoped that someday she would be able to share with a hurting world that God was there even in the deepest of pits.

For thirty-three years, Corrie was able to share this message of hope to thousands of people in more than sixty countries. People believed her because her testimony was forged in the fire of pain and God's grace.

Sarah eventually reached her own point of acceptance. It began when she crumbled to the floor and whispered repeatedly, "No matter what, I trust you, Lord."

With tears, Sarah and her husband's prayerful decision to attend the bar mitzvah placed them on a healing path. Though seats were reserved for them in the family section, she wasn't able to sit so close to all of the festivities, and her tears were a bittersweet mixture of joy and grief. But she stayed.

Later when they returned home, she changed from her party clothes into her bathrobe. She felt a comfortable exhaustion; the contented tiredness of a difficult task well done.

Over time Sarah and the Lord worked through her ragged wound in the Secret Place. She has and continues to be a source of comfort to many women.

This week, as we gently pry open disappointed eyes, let us inquire of the Lord how we can take that first step of acceptance.

Whether we share Sarah's disappointment or the disappointments of the betrayals, lost hopes and dreams, the disillusionment of ministry work, or the frustrated expectations innate to most women, rest assured that in God's eyes every incident is important to him because we are important to him.

Elohey Kol HaNechamah (God of All Encouragement), I'm opening my eyes. And it hurts, like someone who has sat in darkness for a long time and then enters the bright sunlight. But no matter what, Lord, I trust you. *Abba*, as we work on this together, I have hope for the day when I say, "Even though ... yet I will rejoice in the *Lord*." In Yeshua's Name. Amen.

Let's take it to the Secret Place:

What disappointment has taken the breath from my spirit? Have I reconciled my disappointment with the Lord?

_____

_____

_____

Have I ever felt ashamed of my disappointment? If so, why?

_____

_____

_____

Am I ready to accept the disappointment? Am I ready to say, "Yet I will rejoice in the Lord, I will rejoice in the God of my salvation." Why?

_____

_____

_____

End of Week Seven:

Was I able to take my disappointment to the Lord in the Secret Place? Did he minister to me? In what ways?

_____

_____

_____

_____

_____

_____

Week Eight ~ Fearful Eyes

The Snare

The attack began with a blow to the back, followed by a round of hateful obscenities. Before Shoshanna could react, her assailants ran away laughing. They were just kids, two teenage girls who had skipped school and ran the streets, executing random acts of physical violence on unsuspecting passersby. Shoshanna stood alone shaking and wondering what she had done to deserve this.

Shoshanna's body hurt for a few days, but what she didn't know was that a seed of fear had established a place in her. At first, she was able to rationalize the heart palpitations as ordinary nervousness, but the edgy feelings soon came over her anytime she was around a group of teenagers. If she saw young people walking on the sidewalk, she crossed to the other side of the street.

Gradually, the fear infiltrated other areas of her life. She avoided situations where confrontations might occur. Any group participation exhausted her because the entire time she battled inner voices that told her to run and hide. Slowly, she withdrew her involvement in outreach ministries.

Over time, this once gregarious woman found she preferred the safety of isolation.

Fear can infiltrate our souls when we least expect it. Resurfaced circumstances from our childhood or simply reading today's headlines can trigger a stranglehold of apprehension. According to the Anxiety Disorders of America organization, one in thirteen people suffers from some phobia at some point in his or her life. In these end times, the world is programming us for fear. Fear is like a weed; once it overtakes one area of our lives, it moves on to another area.

How can we not fear? Do we have a choice?

Yes.

The Bible calls fear torment (1 John 4:17) and instructs that God has not given us a spirit of fear but one of power, love, and a sound mind (2 Tim. 1:7).

Our Messiah is the *Sar Shalom* (Prince of Peace). Yeshua said, "These things I have spoken to you, that in me you may have peace. In the world you will have tribulation, but be of good cheer, I have overcome the world" (John 16:33). Yeshua makes clear that we will have tribulations and things will "go bump in the night." But his words will give us peace.

So, our peace isn't dependent upon calm circumstances or the avoidance of the things that frighten us. Our peace abides in him. We must choose in those scary moments to trust the Lord.

The Scottish poet Joanna Baillie (1762–1851) wrote:

> The brave [woman] is not [she] who feels no fear,
> For that were stupid and irrational;
> But [she], whose noble soul its fear subdues,
> And bravely dares the danger nature shrinks from

Shoshanna loves the Word of God, and the very isolation that the enemy had pushed her into was the place where she was able to overcome her fear. In her Secret Place, she and the Lord battled through it. God's truth, his grace, and heart-palpitating hard work released her from the stronghold.

Today, Shoshanna's primary ministry is to teenagers—the very age group of her assailants. God has taken her creative gifts into new frontiers: she now writes, directs, and produces wonderful plays with these young people.

There are many types of fear—rejection, disapproval, failure, loneliness, fear of the unknown, fear of the future, and even the fear of succeeding. Whether subtle or obvious, allow the Lord to open our eyes this week and battle this enemy who so easily snares us.

*A*donai Hoshia (Lord of Victory), I know you didn't give me a spirit of bondage to fear; you gave me the Spirit of adoption so that I might call you, Abba (Rom. 8:15).

I know that you haven't given me a spirit of fear but one of power, love, and a sound mind (2 Tim. 1:7).

I know that perfect love casts out all fear (1 John 4:18).

Abba, I know these things in my mind. Your words bring life and peace, but the world, the enemy, my circumstances, and my mind can torment and drain the peace that they provide.

But today, Lord, I choose to reject fear as the lord of my life. I choose to believe in you and your promises. Help me to root out the fear that torments, snares, and keeps me immobile. Give me discerning eyes that can identify these roots and not allow them to grow.

I choose to walk—even with the fear—in the path to which you have called me until I leave that fear behind. In Yeshua's Name. Amen.

Let's take it to the Secret Place:

What frightens me?

_____

_____

_____

How does this fear hold me back?

_____

_____

What could my life look like without this fear?

_____

_____

_____

Am I afraid to take this to the Lord? Why?

_____

_____

End of Week Eight:

Was I able to take my fears to the Lord? How did God speak to me in the Secret Place? In what ways?

_____

_____

_____

_____

Week Nine ~ Calamitous Eyes

Where Were You?

> "Dear friends, don't regard as strange the fiery ordeal occurring among you to test you, as if something extraordinary were happening to you."
>
> I Peters 4:12

She laid her sleeping child in the crib. Unusually fussy that night, the mother breathed a tired sigh and headed for her own bed. She placed her head on the soft pillow in need of rest because tomorrow was going to be another busy day.

But the mother took for granted that the hurricane would bypass their home as others had done in the past. She had no idea that the next day, she would frantically search for her child in the midst of mud and debris—and not find her.

Of all of the tragic Katrina stories, this one struck me the deepest. Why? The obvious chord was that of a mother losing her child, but it was especially distressing because it reminded me that bad things happen to the innocent and guilty alike.

A common question asked by both nonbelievers and believers is why does God allow bad things to happen to good people?

Academically, we can answer this question with the usual, "We live in a fallen world," "God gave us free will," "God is judging a wicked world," and so on. Is this how we would have responded to this mother who lost her infant?

The reality is we have no scriptural guarantees that tomorrow will come for us or that it won't bring with it unthinkable tragedies. Sometimes bad things happen, and we don't know why.

Even the talmidim (disciples) weren't immune from great trials and tribulations or even martyrdom.

Before you put down this week's devotion and wonder why I chose such a depressing topic, please stick with me.

If we can advance past the "why" and tackle the "what next," we can work through the bad things that happen to us and to our loved ones.

God doesn't want our eyes closed in the fear of the innumerable potentials for calamities or misfortunes.

Likewise, he doesn't want us to believe that he is any less in control or in love with us when bad things do happen.

Our Lord wants us to open our eyes, focus on him, and know that he is able and willing to guide us through the most horrendous of difficulties. That is his promise.

Eons ago, when I was a teenager, I tried surfing. I'm a strong swimmer, and the waves didn't seem too large, plus there was a cute guy who was willing to teach me. He suggested that I begin by riding a boogie board on my belly. Later, as I paddled forward to catch a wave, I didn't notice an approaching swell much larger than the previous ones was descending on me. Someone called out to me, and when I looked back, I panicked and forgot everything surfer boy had taught me. The wave swallowed me, shot me down for a mouthful of sand, and then cruelly somersaulted me until I couldn't tell what was top and what was bottom. I was running out of air. Just when I thought that my life was over, a hand grasped my wrist and pulled me to the surface.

When the bad things happen to us and the wave of despair tumbles us mercilessly, God will grasp our hand and pull us to the surface—even if we panic and forget what we've learned.

This week, our assignment is to meditate not on the uncertainty of our fragile lives but on the surety of God's love and comfort. Let's allow the Lord to reveal any areas where our assumptions and expectations keep our eyes closed to the reality of life on this Earth and transfer our focus to understanding of God's great love, grace, and compassion in the midst of these realities.

El Shaddai (God Almighty), you are my refuge and strength; you are there to help me when I'm in trouble. I will not fear even though the earth is removed, the mountains are carried into the midst of the sea, and its waters roar and swirl about me.

I will be still and know that you are God because you are exalted among the nations and on the Earth. You are with me and my refuge when bad things happen (Ps. 46:1–3, 10–11).

I choose to not be afraid of what could come and believe that no matter what might happen to me, you are there and will see me through anything.

Show me this week the exercises that I need to build my faith for the long haul. In Yeshua's Name. Amen.

Let's take it to the Secret Place:

What has been the most difficult event in my history?

_____

_____

_____

_____

How did I respond to it? Did my faith grow stronger? Or did it waver?
Is there anything that I would have done differently? If so, what?

_____

_____

_____

_____

What did the Lord use to bring me back to the surface?

_____

_____

_____

_____

If I haven't surfaced yet, am I able to acknowledge that God is with me in
the middle of this crushing wave? Why?

_____

_____

_____

_____

End of Week Nine:

Did I begin a faith exercise program? How did God speak to me in the Secret Place?

_____

_____

_____

_____

Week Ten ~ Unholy Eyes

Woe Is Me?

> *"Tell [Baruch] that ADONAI says: 'I will tear down what I built up . . .*
> *Are you seeking great things for yourself?' "*
>
> *Jeremiah 45:4,5 (emphasis mine)*

*S*asha had worked for weeks preparing for this gathering of the young people. No one was meeting the needs of this age group in their small congregation, and as usual, she was the someone who could do the job.

She took time off from work to get ready. The house looked beautiful; she'd gathered flowers from her garden and placed them artistically around the living room. The healthy snacks and juices were on the table, ready to welcome the kids.

First, she thought about how she would lead them in prayer and then let them discuss their problems and concerns. Sasha's heart swelled with excitement.

Then, the phone rang. As she ran to answer, she hoped no one was calling to cancel. A few minutes later, Sasha was on the phone, calling parents to cancel the young people's meeting.

She had no idea how much trouble into which her daughter had gotten herself. Now, Sasha had to abandon this ministry, and these young people wouldn't have their needs met. Sasha felt terrible. How could God disappoint these children like this?

Can godly pursuits be unholy and displeasing to God?

The prophet Jeremiah was a man devoted to God and Israel. God required from Jeremiah a solitary life of celibacy. The prophet wrestled with emotional conflict as God gave him one difficult task after another. His own people persecuted him. He saw the downfall of Israel but also received prophecy concerning Israel's future salvation. Jeremiah was an extraordinary man who lived an extraordinary life.

Baruch was Jeremiah's scribe. How exciting it would have been to follow the great Jeremiah on all of his journeys to kings and leaders. Baruch's responsibility was to transcribe the Word of God, spoken to Jeremiah.

Perhaps he dreamed that their team would be like Elijah and Elisha, doing great exploits for the Lord.

Imagine Baruch's disappointment as he scribed words of doom and gloom for Israel, and the people ignored them. Not only did they ignore God's warnings, but the people whom the prophet and scribe had tried to warn persecuted them and took them captive.

Around Baruch is God's judgment and Jeremiah's exhausting efforts, but the scribe bemoaned his disillusionment.

It's easy to picture him, eyes closed and mourning the loss of his dream.

Jeremiah 45 was God's response to Baruch. Jeremiah had to stop his serious pursuits in order to pass on a reprimand to Baruch (and Baruch had to transcribe it):

"Thus, says the LORD, the God of Israel, to you, O Baruch: 'You said, "Woe is me now! For the LORD has added grief to my sorrow. I fainted in my sighing, and I find no rest"' ... Thus, says the LORD: 'Behold, what I have built I will break down, and what I have planted I will pluck up, that is, this whole land. And do you seek great things for yourself? Do not seek them ...'" (vs. 2–5).

Surely, Baruch didn't seek sinful things, and God doesn't necessarily forbid us to seek great things, but we have to keep our pursuits in perspective with God's will and plan.

Sasha learned that while the need for ministry to the young people in her congregation was important and needed, she had missed her most important ministry, her family. Sasha had a long road to repair the damage of her neglect of her daughter, but the Lord was there to guide and comfort her.

God created us women as nurturers. This is a beautiful gift. However, as women, we are susceptible to stretching ourselves too thin with pursuits that are godly but not of God. We also have trouble with priorities in these areas.

In our meditations this week, let's allow the Lord to open our eyes and see if we are neglecting our loved ones, ministry, or business; because if we are, most likely we're also neglecting our relationship with the Lord in favor of other godly pursuits. Let him show us how to focus our attention where he wants in order to truly pursue his will.

Khol L'vavot Doresh (Searcher of All Hearts), I want to do mighty exploits in your Name. Help me to see that my greatest pursuit is my relationship with you and my loved ones. Please reveal any areas where I may be in an unholy pursuit and not pleasing to you. I don't want to work against your plan.

I love you and want to serve you to the best of my ability. Help me to prioritize according to your will. In Yeshua's Name. Amen.

Let's take it to the Secret Place:

Do I have any unholy pursuits? If so, what?

_____

_____

_____

Do I have trouble prioritizing? If so, what are some examples of this?

_____

_____

_____

_____

Am I having a pity party for myself lately? Could I be on an unholy pursuit of greatness?

_____

_____

End of Week Ten:

Was I able to take this to the Lord? How did God speak to me in the Secret Place? In what ways?

_____

_____

_____

_____

_____

Chapter Three

Tired Eyes

*L*ife is busy. All of the timesaving tools that are available to us only seem to create more demands on our time. Then, there are the long-term demands of family and the emotional battles that can drain our hearts and days.

How can we make eye contact with God when we can barely keep our eyes open?

Week Eleven ~ Life-Busyness Eyes

Picture Me Busy

> "... [B]ut those who hope in ADONAI will renew their strength, they will soar aloft as with eagles' wings; when they are running, they won't grow weary, when they are walking, they won't get tired."
>
> Isaiah 40:31

These were to be her golden years with her husband. The nest had finally emptied, and an agenda more like when they were newlyweds stretched before them: quiet evenings alone, leisurely walks through the woods near their home, maybe even candlelight and goblets once in a while. Charlotte had also looked forward to finally having time to expand her radio, speaking, and writing ministries.

But one of their sons had encountered serious marital problems, her three grandchildren needed a stable environment, and her son needed encouragement as he worked through his wife's betrayal. In the middle of the crisis, Charlotte's beloved mother had entered the hospice program, anticipating the end of her earthly life.

Charlotte felt guilty for feeling frustrated. She adored her son, those grandchildren, and her mother. She knew God had called her to care for them. But for nearly thirty years, she'd worked around everyone else's schedule in order to fit in her quiet time and ministry work. She couldn't recall a day when she could simply decide what she wanted to do and do it without interruption.

When her other empty-nester friends spoke of their time in the Secret Place, Charlotte couldn't help feeling jealous. They spoke of cups of their favorite tea next to comfy chairs as worship music played in the background, and of leather-bound journals and women's devotional bibles on their laps. Most days, Charlotte's quiet time was in the car while running errands for her husband, the kids, or her mother. What kind of quiet time was that? Was God pleased with a quickie and nothing more?

What is our quiet time with the Lord supposed to look like? Should it look like a Norman Rockwell picture with comfy furniture and precocious children who gaze in awe while sitting at their mother's feet? Or does it look like thirty minutes of praise and worship, sixty minutes of study, and thirty minutes of prayer—on our knees?

A longtime member of the Billy Graham team had a great-aunt who had a neighbor with fourteen children. Childless herself, the great-aunt was impressed with the mother's gentle and joyous attitude. She asked the mother if she was a spiritual person.

The mother responded that she indeed loved the Lord. The older woman asked how the young mother could spend much quality time with the Lord with all of the racket and confusion around her.

The mother laughed and said, "I have a secret. You notice I wear a big apron. When I want to come apart with the Lord, I just flip the apron over my head and the noise and chatter stops. The children all know that Mother is having her quiet time. I talk to the Lord and have him renew my strength and revive my spirit."[1]

Whether we're busy stay-at-home mothers, busy career women, or both, sometimes we barely have time to shave our legs much less have the picture-perfect quiet time with the Lord.

Question? Who determines what the picture should look like?

This week's passage is simple: wait upon the Lord. Nowhere in the passage does it say where we must wait. It could be while we're waiting to pick up the kids after school. It could be while we're taking the bus to work or waiting for the next meeting to begin. Or while we're waiting in the doctor's office.

The mother with the fourteen children was regularly revived and refreshed by the Lord because she was creative in her waiting places. Although picture-perfect quiet times with the Lord are nice—and I pray all of us can experience them as often as possible—withholding any moment we could spend with the Lord because it's not the customary, ideal time or place is robbing us and the Lord from precious time together.

This week, let's get creative. Find new ways and places to connect with the Lord in the Secret Place. Don't be afraid to try some silly things—like aprons over our heads—because the Lord is anxiously waiting for us.

Dear Lover of my Soul, you know that I want to spend more time with you. You also are well aware of my busy life. So I'm willing to explore new and creative ways of connecting with you in our Secret Place. Thank you that you want to spend time with me and that you miss me—I miss you, too. I'm looking forward to spending more moments with you. In Yeshua's Name. Amen.

Let's take it to the Secret Place:

What would I like my quiet time to look like? Has it ever looked like that? If so, when?

_____

_____

Where do I spend most of my time waiting?

_____

_____

I'm ready to get creative. Where and when could I snatch some moments with the Lord? List them and experiment this week.

_____

_____

_____

_____

End of Week Eleven:

Did I get creative? How did it work out? Was I able to connect with the Lord in new ways? How did God speak to me in the Secret Place?

_____

_____

_____

_____

_____

G.I. Jane

"I am exhausted from crying, my throat is dry and sore, my eyes are worn out with looking for my God."

Psalm 69:3

The babbling stopped, and then Jane heard the familiar sickening thud. She ran to her daughter; her sweet Tovah was seizing. Jane pushed back the guilt for not having been there when the seizure began. Guilt wasted too much of her already depleted energy.

As the loving mother rocked her child, she ground out the prayer of sixteen years, "Oh, God, please help us."

Tovah was diagnosed with pervasive developmental disorder (PDD), a form of autism, at age three. When she was seven, she began having seizures. When Tovah reached puberty, her seizures increased to between eight and nine hundred seizures a month.

There were no warnings and no pre-seizure auras. Even if there were, Tovah couldn't tell her parents because her communication skills were limited. As a result, she fell many times, hitting her head.

Jane has prayed, begged, pleaded, bargained, and even threatened God for her daughter's healing. She's fasted and read the Bible from cover to cover repeatedly. She's asked anyone who prays to remember Tovah. She has even asked complete strangers to pray despite her embarrassment.

The battle-weary mom remembers the day that she decided she was tired of the desperation and the fighting. She wanted to quit this battle—the battle for hope.

What happens when we're too tired to fight? When the battle shows no signs of letting up and there is no end in sight?

When a soldier is trained for battle, he/she must go through basic training. My husband attended Navy boot camp a few months before our wedding. I remember his distressed letters in which he asked for prayer and wondered what in the world he had gotten himself into. Nothing about it seemed civilized, and it was very much in conflict with his polite upbringing.

Preparing a soldier for war requires combat training. The military transforms a young person from a civilian into a fighter ready for battle. America's military trains recruits to work as a team and survive dangerous situations. An individual's life and the lives of those around him or her depend on it.

When we inherit God's blessings through salvation, we also inherit his enemies. Are we properly trained for the spiritual battles of life and ministry? Are we trained for the practical battles that we fight each day in bad marriages, in frustrating jobs, with sick children, in loneliness, through poor health, or during financial challenges? An ill-equipped soldier is more likely to be wounded.

I believe Jane was and is a well-trained warrior. Her dedicated heart to the Lord and her family is well known. She has a strong testimony. So why was she weary? She was weary because the battle was protracted and intense, and she realized it could continue for an extended period of time—perhaps a lifetime.

Jane's mutiny didn't last long. She hadn't realized how much the Lord had sustained her until she had stopped seeking his strength. During this brief insubordination, she had a dream. She felt a hand shake her, and a voice said, "Watch and pray so you will not fall into temptation. The spirit is willing, but the body is weak."

The admonition didn't discourage her; it empowered her because she was truly a soldier. She understood what it meant to be a warrior and knew she couldn't be victorious without fighting the battle. And she does—every day.

Are we trained and battle-ready? Have we been wounded so many times in battle that we don't want to go back and fight? Are we weary and losing heart in fighting the battles that the Lord has assigned us?

This week, let's ask the Lord what type of soldier we are. Are we well trained and battle-ready? Are we poorly trained and easily wounded? Are we well trained but battle-weary? Let's look to our Commander for instruction and encouragement—and perhaps a necessary admonition.

My Commander, my Hope, my Father—what type of soldier am I? Do I understand what it takes to fight the battles that I'm called to? Lord, I'm ready to learn to fight according to your training and battle plans.

I won't grow weary while doing good because in due season, I will reap, provided I don't lose heart (Gal. 6:9). Train me up in your ways, and I won't depart from them (Prov. 22:6). And remind me each day to put on my full armor as I do battle (Eph. 6:10–20). Open my tired eyes to trust you as I train and battle. In Yeshua's Name. Amen.

And p.s., Yeshua, as the Captain of the Hosts, if you can spare a few angels, I wouldn't mind some reinforcements. In your Name. Amen.

Let's take it to the Secret Place:

What type of soldier am I? Am I satisfied with this? Why?

_____

_____

What are my most difficult battles? Am I battling them with the tools God has given me or my own?

_____

_____

Am I battle-weary, wounded, or ill equipped to fight? Do I know the plan to restore my place in battle?

_____

_____

_____

_____

End of Week Twelve:

Did I hear from the Lord about the type of soldier I am? What were his orders? Was I able to take my concerns about this to him in the Secret Place? What did he say?

_____

_____

_____

_____

_____

Week Thirteen ~ Defeated Eyes

God's Novel

> "... [L]ooking unto [Yeshua], the author and finisher of our faith, who for the joy that was set before him endured the cross, despising the same, and has sat down at the right hand of the throne of God."
>
> Hebrews 12:2 (NKJV)

Angie sat before her boss—the familiar voices of inadequacy and rejection taunted her. Her shaking hands folded in her lap as she raised her eyes to meet her employer's.

"I think you need to find someone else to take my job," she said.

Her boss's head jerked like she'd taken a swing at him.

"Why?"

Angie swallowed.

"Because I think you could do better. I'm always struggling. I'm not well educated. You need someone in this position with a degree or something."

A smile replaced his look of surprise. He shook his head and chuckled.

"So you're really willing to give up on the department you've worked so hard to build?"

It was Angie's turn to be surprised.

"I'm not giving up! I'm—"

Was she giving up? Why?

Are we willing to walk away in defeat before we fight?

There's a little sticky note on my desk that long ago lost its stickiness. With its curling edges and faded color, you'd think I would have transferred the information to a fresher note. However, the shabby appearance seems to punctuate the words written on it:

Convincing
Characters
Caught in
Compelling
Conflict

The alliteration was meant to instruct new writers in the art of writing novels, but it has come to mean so much more to me.

A novelist must put her characters through great conflict in order for her story to be interesting. If there are no conflicts, the story and characters are boring, one-dimensional, and of little interest to a reader. The novelist's message or theme is impotent unless the character goes through the realization and then struggles to overcome his or her weaknesses.

The Scripture says that Yeshua is our author. In a sense, we are his living novels. He has implanted a message of hope to this world in each of us. Are we worth reading? Are we convincing characters overcoming compelling conflicts, or do we give up at the first sight of conflict?

Yeshua is also the finisher of our faith. When I think of finishing, I think of the final polish a carpenter puts on a beautiful piece of new furniture. The hard rubbing produces a finish that invites the touch of interested buyers.

Does our life shine with the obvious touch of Yeshua? Or do we avoid his hand? What keeps us from pushing through to victory? How easily do we give up in defeat when it comes to our ministries, weight, jobs, marriages, friendships, faults, or sins?

Angie sat in front of her boss and argued with herself. "I want to stay and continue to build this department. But how can I when I'm not qualified? But how could I not be qualified when God called me and trained me himself? But what if God didn't really call me?" The confused woman looked toward her boss.

The man gave her a compassionate what-are-you-stupid-of-course-he-has-called-you look. Her cheeks flamed. Yes, God had called her. After eight years in the job, how could she not know that?

Angie continues to struggle with the compelling conflicts that make her a convincing character in God's story. Despite the frustration—or maybe because of it—she knows she's where she is called. She prays that Yeshua's touch shines in her life and that others might be drawn to him.

Let's explore our character this week. Are we convincing in our testimonies? Do we shine with Yeshua's hand-rubbed touch? Are we putting aside fear and meeting compelling conflicts head on?

By the way, God has already completed our story. I'm sure I'm not spoiling it for you when I say it's a very happily-ever-after ending.

Dear Lord, I've never thought of my life as your story; that Yeshua authored and finished my faith. I want to be a convincing character and not run from the conflicts of my life. Please begin to show me how to do that this week. In my Author and Finisher's Name. Amen.

Let's take it to the Secret Place:

What kind of character am I?

_____

_____

What are my compelling conflicts in life?

_____

_____

_____

Do I run from the conflicts? If so, why?

_____

_____

_____

_____

End of Week Thirteen:

What did I learn about my character this week? Did I take my defeat to the Lord in the Secret Place? What did he say?

_____

_____

_____

_____

_____

_____

Week Fourteen ~ Overwhelmed Eyes

Who's the Biggest?

> "Moshe [Moses] said to ADONAI, 'Oh, ADONAI, I'm a terrible speaker. I always have been and I'm no better now, even after you've spoken to your servant! My words come slowly, my tongue moves slowly.' ADONAI answered him, 'Who gives a person a mouth? Who makes a person dumb or deaf, keen-sighted or blind? Isn't it I, ADONAI? Now, therefore go; and I will be with your mouth and will teach you what to say.'"
>
> Exodus 4:10-12

Joella's body tensed as the rabbi's wife approached her. Dread spread through her body like an oil spill from a tanker. Although Joella had known this moment would come—God had warned her it would—her mind had geared up with a list of excuses to avoid it.

Minutes later, every excuse had evaporated from Joella's mind, and all that she had managed to say was a timid okay.

One little word had shifted her from predictability to the unknown, overwhelming world of public speaking. In three weeks, she would stand before a room full of women at their congregation's retreat.

For the next three weeks, Joella built a circus of fear. In the center ring was every insecure thought that she'd ever known: I'm not smart enough; I'm not pretty enough; I have a squeaky voice; I have a very strong East Coast accent; I never know what I might say that will embarrass our leadership or the Lord; my health isn't good; what if I have a heart attack or stroke while I'm at the podium? What in the world is the Lord thinking?

Is the Lord calling you to something that is outside your comfort zone? Have you worked yourself into such a frenzy of fear that you're exhausted and ready to give up?

On the eve of battle, the prophet Elisha's servant panicked when the enemy had encamped around the city. This servant had witnessed numerous miracles that God had performed through Elisha, but the insurmountable odds and their defensive inadequacies were too much for the young man.

> *"Oh, my master, this is terrible! What are we going to do?" [Elisha] answered, "Don't be afraid—those who are with us outnumber those who are with them!" Elisha prayed, "ADONAI, I ask you to open his eyes, so that he can see." Then ADONAI opened the young man's eyes, and he saw; there before him, all around Elisha, the mountain was covered with horses and fiery chariots.*
>
> *(2 Kings 6:15b—18)*

The young servant's vision of God was much smaller than Elisha's was.

The evening before Joella was to speak all of her doubts, fears, and insecurities felt like an elephant was sitting on her chest. The pressure to her head had her convinced she would have a stroke. Joella knew she needed to pray. She had her own servant conversation with the Lord; it went like this:

Joella: I can't do this.

God: I'm not sending you to your execution.

Joella: Oh, you can send me there. At least I'll be with you after I'm executed.

God: All I have asked of you is to take my words and speak them.

Joella: What if I disappoint you? I'm nobody.

God: Actually you're too big. You're in my way.

Joella: What? I'm afraid.

God: Fear Me.

Fear Me. Those two words put the tumult of emotions into perspective. Joella had exalted her fears, insecurities, and frailties above the knowledge and grace of God—the very One who had called her to speak. The task was not too big; she was.

The next day, Joella spoke the words God had given her to speak years before. She had a beautiful life-changing experience, but that story is for later (see Week 48).

God may be calling you out of your comfort zone and into something new. Maybe it's taking a class, asking for that promotion, teaching a Shabbat (Sabbath) school class, or joining the next outreach event. Let's explore any new directions that the Lord might be taking us in the Secret Place, and trust that he is bigger than our fears.

M'falti (My Deliverer), I'm nervous, but I don't want to be. If you are leading me in a new direction or asking me to try something new, I don't want to stand in the way. It's easy for me to feel overwhelmed when I think of my inadequacies. Help me to remember you are a big God. In my Yeshua's Name. Amen.

Let's take it to the Secret Place:

Is there something the Lord has wanted me to do? If so, what?

_____

_____

What is keeping me from pursuing this?

_____

_____

Is there something he wants me to do to prepare? If so, what?

_____

_____

_____

_____

Do I have a goal in mind? Is there a trusted prayer partner with whom I can share this?

_____

_____

End of Week Fourteen:

Was I able to take my bigness to the Lord in the Secret Place? What did he say?

_____

_____

_____

Week Fifteen~Self-Imposed Busyness Eyes

No, Thank You

> *"Moshe's father-in-law said to him, 'What you are doing isn't good. You will certainly wear yourself out—and not only yourself, but these people here with you as well. It's too much for you—you can't do it alone, by yourself.'"*
>
> *Exodus 18:17—18*

There was a point in my life where I wondered if my headstone would read: "Here lies Terri: Absent wife and mother, died young because she couldn't say no." Sometimes I sing a silly anthem, "Can't Say No."² Feel free to join in.

> *I'm jist a girl who cain't say no,*
> *I'm in a turrible fix*
> *I always say, "For sure, I'll go,"*
> *Jist when I orta say nix!*
> *It ain't so much a question of what I cain or cain't do.*
> *I knowed there's only twenty-fer hours in a day, nu?³*
> *I heared a lot of stories, and I reckon they are true*
> *'Bout how girls cain do anythin' they put their mind to.*
> *But does they have to do 'em all 'stead of one or two?*
> *I'm jist a girl who cain't say no,*
> *No matter what it costs.*
> *I hate to disserpoint a soul*
> *Even tho I'm ready to plotz!⁴*

The sisters Miriam (Mary) and Marta (Martha) embody the ageless struggle for women of faith. Miriam's eyes were fixed on Yeshua, but Marta's were on the seemingly compulsory tasks before her.

What are some of the reasons we take on more than we should?

1. It feels good. That first flush of gratitude from the person in need can be addictive.
2. I said, "Yes," before I realized it. Even when we regret it, we're too embarrassed to say so.
3. I misjudged the time it would take. If we are inexperienced or don't take the time to get the complete picture, we can misjudge how much time a project or task can take.
4. No one else will do it. This is probably one of the most deceptive schemes of the enemy. If we are not called to do this task and God wants it done, we are robbing someone else from the blessing of doing it.
5. No one else can do it. Another ploy of the enemy that appeals to our pride.
6. Avoidance of other responsibilities. If we crave validation, our mundane, repetitive responsibilities seldom meet that yearning. It's much more rewarding to seek outside recognition for our efforts.
7. Seeking distraction from our own problems. Although stepping outside our own problems to help others can be a healthy activity, the problem arises when we use the activity to avoid dealing with our own issues.
8. We do it all ourselves. Sometimes a task is too big for one person. Are we patient enough to guide others to share the task? Or is it difficult to share the recognition?

How can we avoid these snares? First, if we are prone to saying yes, start by stating, "Let me get back to you," or, "Let me pray about it."

If we are positioned like Miriam—at the feet of Yeshua, we are less likely to be confused or allow our minds to be swayed toward projects that sidetrack us from our responsibilities or relationships.

However, sometimes even after prayer, it's not clear if we should say yes or no. Like Moshe, we should seek wise counsel from our leadership or friends who know us well and are mature in the Lord.

I'm better at saying no. And I'm also better at delegating responsibilities. It only took about forty-five years to get there. I'm also learning that I shouldn't depend on others, but on the Lord, for my validation.

This week, let's focus our tired, self-imposed busyness eyes on the Lord. Maybe we could make a commitment to not take on a new project or outside responsibility for this week. Then, take the time we have saved to allow the Lord to strengthen our discernment and confidence to say no!

Lord, I'm tired of being a girl who can't say no. Please open my eyes to the areas where I'm taking on more than I should. Please, Lord, I need to build my discernment muscles and not be afraid to say no. In Yeshua's Name. Amen.

Let's take it to the Secret Place:

What percent of me is a Marta? Do I need regular validation in my life? Explain.

_____

_____

_____

_____

Is it difficult for me to say no to someone in need? What are my usual reasons for this?

_____

_____

_____

_____

How can I practice saying no? Am I able to do this prayerfully?

_____

_____

_____

_____

End of Week Fifteen:

Did I take my need to pile on busyness to the Lord in the Secret Place? What did he say?

_____

_____

_____

Chapter Four

Hardened Eyes

Hardened eyes can be a sign of a hardened heart. Is it possible to not know that we have hardened our heart?

During the next five weeks, let's prayerfully examine our eyes to be sure that they are not immovable, hidden, prideful, unforgiving, and/or divisive. If any part of our heart has hardened, we'll take it to the Lord in the Secret Place. He loves softening hearts.

Week Sixteen ~ Immovable Eyes

Someone Call the Waambulance!

> "There in the desert the whole community of the people of Isra'el grumbled against Moshe and Aharon [Aaron]."
>
> Exodus 16:2

In 2000, Disney released a movie called *The Kid*, which starred Bruce Willis as a high-powered Hollywood public image consultant who had little patience with whiners. If someone cried or whined around him, he said, "Waaa! Someone call the waambulance."

Can whining be more than an annoying habit? What are we saying when we grumble or murmur about our circumstances?

Jan Silvious' book, Big Girl's Don't Whine cautions women against the little girl ways that we sometimes can use to manipulate others. How many times have we whined, complained, moaned, or pouted until our intended victim gave in to our desires? Or worse, how many times has our criticizing and griping caused division in our homes, congregations, or offices?

The reality is even if we control our intended target or gather an army of fellow dissidents, have we really won? What if pouting and whining to get our way actually pushes us away from our Abba?

The Hebrew word for murmur is *luwn*. The word picture implies a person who chooses to stay permanently in a place, be obstinate, or hold a grudge for a long period.

Doesn't being obstinate or immovable sound like something more akin to rebellion?

Difficult challenges await us daily. Generally most of us need time to process a deep hurt, difficult task, or crisis that comes into our lives. Being able to talk to others and pray through the trouble or frustration is healthy. But at some point, we need to release the emotions to the Lord and allow him to provide the emotional/spiritual healing that we need to move forward with him—even if there is no physical healing or satisfying resolution to our trials.

What is the tipping point from processing to murmuring, whining, and complaining? Based on the Hebrew definition, it's when we can't move past that point of pain or offense. Our eyes become hardened with rebellion.

The opposite of rebellion is faith. We need faith to be obedient.

This week, let's allow the Lord to open both our eyes and our ears. Do we have trouble hearing our own tone of voice? Perhaps finding someone who can honestly assess when we whine, grumble, or murmur will help us begin to overcome this sin.

Do we hear that whine in our voice, the long sighs, or the grumbles that we deposit on others about injustices toward us or other people?

Maybe it's time to watch for the waambulance. If we hear the whine, look in the mirror and check for hardened eyes.

El Rachum (Merciful God), you know I don't want to have rebellious eyes. You know my heart.

I repent of my murmuring, grumbling, and whining. Thank you for your grace and mercy.

This week, reveal the areas where I tend to be immovable or where I whine, grumble, or complain to get my own way.

Please sensitize me so that I can hear the whine of the waambulance. I don't want to be immovable, but I want to move away from my sin toward you. I believe. Help me with my unbelief. In Yeshua's Name. Amen.

Let's take it to the Secret Place:

Am I a chronic or occasional whiner? Is there a difference? Why?

_____

_____

_____

How does whining, grumbling, or murmuring affect my body? My tone of voice? My attitude?

_____

_____

_____

_____

Where are my whine zones? My home? The congregation? My office? The car?

_____

_____

_____

_____

End of Week Sixteen:

What did I learn about my whining and murmuring? How did God speak to me in the Secret Place? How has our relationship improved?

_____

_____

_____

Week Seventeen ~ Hidden Eyes

Hiding in Plain Site

"[She] who conceals [her] sins will not succeed; [she] who confesses and abandons them will gain mercy."

Proverbs 28:13

hocolate sauce was smeared on nearly every kitchen surface within a two-year-old's reach. Little Robby sat in the middle of the mess covered in goo with his hands behind his back.

Once the mother downshifted her anger to a toddler's level, she asked him a simple question, "Did you make this mess, Robby?"

After a little flutter of his long lashes, Robby's big brown eyes enlarged and moistened to a well-rehearsed innocence.

"No, mommy." A small glob of chocolate dropped from his hair. "I wub you so much."

Have we ever tried to hide our sin from the Lord?

Most of us reading this devotional know that we can't hide our sins from God (Ps. 69:5, Ps. 139, Acts 5:1–11). He sees into our very souls, no matter how like little Robby we might try.

Today, sitting in congregations, serving in ministries, and attending prayer meetings and Bible studies around the world are people who are hiding from God in plain sight.

According to a 2005 Barna study, only eighteen percent of people polled said that completely understanding and carrying out the principles of their faith was the highest priority in their lives (fourteen percent of men versus eighteen percent of women).[1] That means more than eighty percent of believers don't hold God's principles as their highest priority. Having a satisfying family life scored top honors. Although that's a worthy goal, the study sends a red flag. Our priorities are off-balance.

Like Robby, do we think because we are God's child and we say we love him that we can get away with our sin? What might hiding from God in plain sight look like?

Alona is active in her synagogue and the women's prayer and Bible meetings. Sitting together during Shabbat services, Alona, her husband, and two children are picture perfect. She lifts her hands and dances during praise and worship. But at night, after everyone has gone to sleep, she meets with her new online "friend." It's not physical; she's never met the man. Alona used to feel the tightening in her chest and stomach that signaled maybe it wasn't right, but that conviction is rare now.

Dova is generally the first to volunteer for nearly every congregational need. Her harried face is the first that people see at services and the last as she tidies up the sanctuary. Dova doesn't have time for friendships, the close kind anyway. Everyone marvels at how she shuns attention or recognition. But the truth is Dova has been shoplifting for years. Little things she needs for the house and the kids. When she does it and after the adrenaline rush subsides, Dova feels the oppressive weight of guilt and thinks that she probably shouldn't have done it. But she just volunteers for another task at the synagogue and feels better. God wouldn't hold her accountable, especially not publicly, because of all she does for him, would he?

Are we guilty of similar sins? Of hardening our hearts to the prevalent conviction God offers in our services, prayer meetings, and Bible studies, as well as our Secret Place?

Maybe we think because our sins are smaller, like holding grudges, taking office supplies home, or cheating on our taxes. They aren't as big as Alona's or Dova's sins. It's okay to ignore the tightening of our guts or the heat in our chests, right?

God uses his Holy Spirit to alert us to unrepentant sin. Each of us knows what that feels like physically and spiritually. When we ignore the warnings, we harden our hearts, the sin is not repented, and, therefore, it is not forgiven. Leaving our Secret Place with our hearts unclean by choice means we have hardened our eyes to his probing gaze.

If this makes us uncomfortable, then praise the Lord! Our loving Abba's conviction is doing its job.

This week, let's pay special attention to God's warning signals of conviction. If part of our heart has hardened, we can pray this prayer, and God will turn our hearts of stone to hearts of flesh. He doesn't want to punish us—though there may be consequences for which we are accountable—he wants to love on us freely.

El Nosey (Forgiving God), I repent of _____. I want to get right with you. A part of me is hardened, and I'm afraid it will spread to other areas in my life. By your Ruach (Spirit), convict me of any other sin that keeps me from you. If I have to make some things right, Abba, thank you for standing by me as I account for them. I trust you. In Yeshua's Name. Amen.

Let's take it to the Secret Place:

Are there sins in my life that I'm hiding in plain sight? What are they?

_____

_____

_____

_____

How long have I hardened my eyes to God's gaze? Why?

_____

_____

_____

_____

Do I need to find someone I trust to discuss this with? What consequences do I expect for my actions?

_____

_____

_____

_____

Do I trust the Lord's love and forgiveness to enter the Secret Place and begin working through these sins? Why?

_____

_____

_____

End of Week Seventeen:

How did God speak to me in the Secret Place? Am I still hiding in plain sight? How has our relationship improved?

_____

_____

_____

_____

Week Eighteen~ Prideful Eyes

What's That?!

> *"How can you say to your [sister], 'Let me take the splinter out of your eye,' when you have the log in your own eye?'"*
>
> Matthew 7:4

O nce I made the mistake of asking God what my pride looked like to him. (Okay, so I wasn't thinking.) He began with an aerial view of what appeared to be an empty throne nestled in the clouds. As I drew nearer, I could see from the back that it was draped in rich tapestries, gold, and jewels.

"That must be God's throne!" I thought.

Like a movie camera zooming in closer, the visual panned to the front of the empty chair and focused on something tiny on the seat.

"What could it be?"

As I drew nearer, I recognized the little brown things. I could identify them because our daughter's Chihuahua puppy, Paco, had left these little brown droppings around the house.

My pride looked like Paco's poop on God's throne? Ew.

Fortunately, God and I have this type of relationship. He'll sometimes take very serious issues and add a little humor so the lesson is easier to swallow. I certainly remember it better. What was most grave about this picture was that the throne represented God's throne in my heart. Not only was he not sitting in his rightful place, but I'd replaced him with dog poop.

Most of us recognize what I'd call "obvious pride": looking down on someone because they're poor or not as educated, always wanting to be in the limelight or the center of attention, or interrupting people or not listening to other opinions are a few examples.

I'm confident that we all take these sinful behaviors seriously and work on them; however, I'd like to address a not-so-obvious type of pride—criticizing.

Excluding constructive criticism (which I'm not convinced truly exists) or solicited analysis, most criticism is our fleshy attempt at doing the Holy Spirit's job. Many of us want to point out people's faults, mistakes, or sins. We want to be the one who convicts. But do we offer a sense of release and restoration, or is it our attempt to produce more proof that we're better than the other person? Perhaps the evidence is whether our relationship with the person afterward is stronger or strained?

Our scripture this week is Yeshua's familiar parable of pointing out the splinter in someone else's eye when there is a whole log in our own.

Oswald Chambers, in *My Utmost for His Highest*, postulates that when we see a speck in someone's eye, it's most likely the first inkling that there is a wooden beam in our own eye. Our pride has camouflaged it from us.

Have our prideful eyes caused us to miss our significant flaws?

The Holy Spirit's job is to convict us. He does it with the intent of our seeking restoration and freedom from sin's bondage. He takes no pleasure in hurting or wounding us.

This week, let's ask the Lord to show us if we've replaced him with poop on the thrones of our hearts. Let's also pay closer attention to our attitudes with others. Are we regularly critical of others? Do we point out the splinters in their eyes when there's a sequoia in ours?

Yoshev (Enthroned One), by your Ruach HaKodesh (Holy Spirit) reveal any logs in my eye, beginning with the pride that keeps me from seeing these logs. Sensitize my eyes to foreign objects that keep them hardened from your truth. I know you love me. You show me these difficult truths so that I can be set free. Thank you. In Yeshua's Name. Amen.

Let's take it to the Secret Place:

Is God sitting on his throne in my heart? Why or why not?

_____

_____

_____

_____

Do I tend to point out others' mistakes, flaws, or sins? Why?

_____

_____

Was I needlessly critical last week? Last month? Today?
If so, give examples.

_____

_____

_____

_____

Are there any damaged relationships because of my criticism?
If so, am I ready to repent and attempt to reconcile the relationships?

_____

_____

_____

_____

Was I able to begin cleaning off God's throne of anything that doesn't belong there? How did God speak to me in the Secret Place? How has our relationship improved?

_____

_____

_____

_____

Week Nineteen ~ Unforgiving Eyes

Onions

> "'I forgave you all that debt because you begged me. Should you not also have had compassion on your fellow servant, just as I had pity on you?' And his master was angry, and delivered him to the torturers until he should pay all that was due to him."
>
> *Matthew 18:32b-34 (NKJV)*

The ugly brown spot was deeper than I thought. After peeling several layers of the onion, my eyes looked like a waterfall.

Forgiveness is like an onion: lots of tears until we finally get through all of the layers.

Has someone ever said that they forgave you, but their tone of voice, body language, and lack of eye contact contradicted their words? You didn't feel forgiven, did you? Have you ever done the same?

Unforgiveness is probably the easiest sin to which we can harden our hearts. During the course of a normal day, we've probably had to formally or informally forgive someone at least once. If it's a particularly trying day, the forgiveness queue can be as long as the Friday afternoon express line at the grocery store.

But what of the big hurts—betrayal, rape, abuse, or unwarranted accusations? How do we forgive something that brutal?

In Matthew 18, Yeshua set a precedent for whom we should forgive. We must forgive anyone, whether he or she asks or even is not repentant. In fact, it is a prerequisite of God's forgiveness to us (Matt. 6:14, 15; Luke 11:4; James 2:13).

Our example of forgiveness is our Heavenly Father:

1. His forgiveness is always available (Ps. 86:5; 1 John 1:9).
2. Forgiveness cost him—we have forgiveness because of the torture and death of Yeshua (Isa. 53:3–10).

3. With God's forgiveness, he remembers our sins no more (Jer. 31:31–34; Heb. 8:12; 10:17).
4. When God forgives, he restores fellowship (Rom. 5:11).

The onion analogy is like God's example of the forgiveness process. What could this look like for us?

1. Being ready for forgiveness. When we have a deep respect for God's forgiveness of us, we can prepare our hearts for the difficult task of forgiving the big hurts. Remember Yeshua's pattern for prayer, "Forgive us our sins as we forgive those who have sinned against us." Does this mean we can do it immediately? Probably not. At some point, whether or not we feel the forgiveness, we must choose to forgive.
2. Forgiveness will cost us. The world tells us to take revenge on those who hurt our loved ones or us. God tells us not to. The world wants us to broadcast the offense to whomever will listen and disparage the offender. God says we must give up that right. Even if we are called to testify in court, our testimony must be accurate without embellishment.
3. Short of a lobotomy or brainwashing, we might find it difficult not to remember the sin. Perhaps God wants us to train our minds to not meditate or discuss the offense or offender unless absolutely necessary. Perhaps it means we surrender our right to bring it to God again and again.
4. Restoring fellowship isn't always practical or safe. In most instances, however, we should be able to work through rebuilding the relationship. If you question whether this is safe or prudent, seek out the Lord in the Secret Place, and then go to your leadership for confirmation. There are extraordinary testimonies of miraculous restorations, such as Stephen Saint whose close relationship with his father's murderer was the subject of the movie Edge of the Spear. The result was whole villages came to salvation.

Sometimes it takes a long time to peel back all of the layers of forgiveness. But incomplete forgiveness of someone can cause a hardening of our hearts, and according to Matthew 18:34, we will experience spiritual torture.

Let's carefully examine God's pattern for forgiveness and compare it to our own. If we need to peel away more of the onion, let's begin this week.

El Rachum (Merciful God), thank you for your forgiveness. I know it cost you and *Yeshua* much pain. I don't want to take your forgiveness in vain by not forgiving others. *Lord*, by your *Ruach Hakodesh (Holy Spirit)* reveal if there are still layers of the onion that I need to remove from my life. You are about reconciliation. Help me to partner with you, according to your will and guidance. In *Yeshua's Name. Amen.*

Let's take it to the Secret Place:

Do I have a whole or partial onion that I need to peel away? Explain.

_____

_____

_____

_____

_____

Am I ready to forgive? Why or why not?

_____

_____

_____

How much will this forgiveness cost me? Explain.

_____

_____

_____

_____

After forgiving someone, do I still bring up the offense and offender? If I do, to whom do I bring it up? Why?

_____

_____

_____

_____

End of Week Nineteen:

Was I able to begin peeling back the layers of forgiveness? How did God speak to me about this in the Secret Place? How has our relationship improved?

_____

_____

_____

_____

Week Twenty ~ Divisive Eyes

Divided and We're Conquered

> "... I urge you, [sisters], to watch out for those who cause divisions and put snares alongside the teaching in which you have been trained—keep away from them."
>
> Romans 16:17

> "Warn a divisive person once, then a second time, and after that, have nothing more to do with [her]."
>
> Titus 3:10

*J*ennifer looked up from her budget reports as Gloria, one of her staff, walked into her office. Gloria seemed agitated as she informed Jennifer that some of the other employees were upset because of all the computer problems. Jennifer assured her the technical staff was busy working on the problem and that she appreciated Gloria and the other employees' patience. The two chitchatted a little more before Gloria thanked her and went back to work. Jennifer was encouraged to have such a dependable employee like Gloria, especially with all of the challenges lately.

Later, Jennifer left her office to get a cup of coffee. As she stirred in the cream, she overheard Gloria speaking with several of the other staff.

"She said they were working on the problems, but I've heard that before," Gloria said.

The supervisor heard a few murmurs of agreement. Now, in addition to the computer problems, Jennifer had people problems weighing on her, too.

Causing disunity may be the most dangerous of sins to the body of Messiah. The first divisive event began with Satan. Not only did he rebel against God, but he took a group of angels with him. He established a pattern for division: rebelling against authority and drawing others away.

One of the seven sins that God hates is disunity (Prov. 6:19). In addition to the concept of stirring others to rebel against his authority,

God also abhors another type of division, those who cause division between others.

"A worthless person digs up evil [gossip]—it is like scorching fire on [her] lips. A deceitful person stirs up strife, and a slanderer can separate even close friends" (Prov. 16:27–28).

Most of us don't think of ourselves as "dividers"; however, many of us have spread of seeds of division:

1. Speaking against leadership, employers, or spouses, especially in group settings.
2. Being attracted to discussions about others.
3. Using duplicity like Gloria.
4. Becoming easily offended and struggling to forgive and let go of the offense.
5. Being easily drawn into others' criticism of individuals.
6. Nitpicking the rabbi's sermon, your boss's directives, or spouse's conversations.

This week's passages are strong admonitions against people who are prone to causing strife and division. God wants us to notice them, and then if, after correction, they continue in their sin, God says we are to reject them. I don't think we want to be included in that exclusive club.

This week's spiritual eye exam is both sobering and critical. Are we ready to allow the Holy Spirit to examine and test us for divisive eyes? Let's pay special attention to behaviors that might be divisive and work extra hard at fostering unity.

El Ro'i (God who sees), please, please, Lord, keep me from having divisive eyes. I don't want to come between my sisters or anyone in the body of Messiah. By your Ruach HaKodesh (Holy Spirit), please open my eyes to any behaviors that cause disunity. If I have participated in these behaviors, please forgive me. Teach me to promote unity. In Yeshua's Name. Amen.

Let's take it to the Secret Place:

Have I been guilty of divisive behaviors? If so, what are my weak areas?

_____

_____

_____

Have I ever contributed to a split of a friendship, congregation, ministry, or business? How does this compare with the Scriptures and lessons above?

_____

_____

_____

_____

What are ways I can promote unity in my congregation? My home? My job?

_____

_____

_____

_____

End of Week Twenty:

How was this week's eye exam? Did the Lord reveal areas I need to work on in the Secret Place? How has our relationship improved?

_____

_____

_____

Chapter Five

Unhealthy Eyes

*H*ave you ever had an eye infection? Some eye conditions are a sign of greater problems, like diabetes or heart conditions. Spiritually, an unhealthy set of eyes can be a sign of another type of heart disease—sin. Is it possible we don't realize just how unhealthy we are?

Let's prayerfully examine ourselves for eyes that are unclean, blurred, dry, or envious—unhealthy conditions that can restrict our view of God.

Week Twenty-One ~ Unclean Eyes

Time to Clean the Pond Filter

> *"Turn my eyes away from worthless things; with your ways, give me life."*
> Psalms 119:37

Tucked within the wisteria of our backyard was a small fishpond. My husband installed a filter that had a little fountain attachment. The fish benefited from a cleaner pond, and we received enjoyment from listening to the water's soothing sounds on warm summer nights.

With all of these praiseworthy benefits came responsibilities. The filter required cleaning every day. It was a messy, smelly chore. Without the daily cleaning, the algae clogged the filter and only a small trickle of water came through the fountainhead. If we procrastinated longer, it stopped working completely and the pond looked like a breeding ground for malaria.

Our spirits also need a filter. Two of those filters are our physical eyes and the eyes of our hearts (Eph. 1:18). If our filters aren't working properly—screening out the impurities of life—God's fountain of living waters can be disrupted or stopped altogether. How can we see the Lord when our eyes are unclean?

The book *Every Man's Battle* by Stephen Arterburn, Fred Stoeker, and Mike Yorkey is a guide to help men overcome sexual temptation. One of the first steps recommended is for men to make a covenant with their eyes, based on Job 31:1, "I will make a covenant with my eyes not to let them lust after any girl."

Can women also struggle with a lust problem?

Kyla enjoyed her new friend and business partner, Lily. She had met the young mother at a craft store. They had struck up a conversation and brainstormed a new business venture in the course of an hour. Kyla's friend was funny, smart, and talented.

The two women met several evenings a week to work on their product. Their husbands babysat while the ladies worked in the basement/gallery of Kyla's home.

They chatted about any number of topics and laughed.

Sometimes the conversations about men were earthy, but it was just between them.

Kyla loved Lily's witty sense of humor. She especially loved hearing her friend's observations of the grocery store's new produce guy's tush (rear end). At times, Kyla's stomach ached from all of the laughter.

Lately, Lily had shared funny conversations between her and the man that had included risqué double entendre. Kyla was a little uncomfortable with the shift in the interaction between her friend and the produce man. Yet, Kyla was also a little curious and began frequenting her friend's grocery store rather than the one where she normally shopped. She found she took pleasure in watching him and some of the other handsome men there.

One afternoon, she happened upon her friend and the produce man holding hands in the organic vegetable section.

One month later, Lily left town with the produce man. She also left behind a confused husband and three devastated children. Kyla couldn't look Lily's husband in the eye, especially when he had asked if she had known how long the affair had been going on.

Different sources place extramarital affairs among women between twenty and forty percent. Nearly eighty percent of young women who pledge to remain virgins until marriage don't.

Today, images and words that would have rightly been considered pornography to our grandparents assault our eyes. Marketing pundits advise companies to push the television censors' limits.

Are we reading sensual secular romance novels? Are we watching movies at home or the theater that make us uncomfortable? Are we reading magazines that promote values that conflict with God's Word? Is it time we made a covenant with our physical and spiritual eyes?

This week, let's take a look at our filters to see if they need cleaning. Are there images floating around in our minds that wage war with biblical principles? Are we ready to make that covenant with our eyes? There's no better place to do that than in the Secret Place with the Lord.

Dear Lord, please forgive me for _____. I'm choosing to turn my eyes away from worthless things because your ways give me life. Help me to make that covenant with my eyes. I don't want anything to come between us. I love you. Thank you for your love and mercy. In Yeshua's Name. Amen.

Let's take it to the Secret Place:

When was the last time that I cleaned out my filter? What have I allowed into my mind lately?

_____

_____

_____

What does making a covenant with my eyes mean practically to me? How will it affect my life?

_____

_____

_____

_____

_____

Am I ready to make the covenant now? Why or why not?

_____

_____

_____

End of Week Twenty-One:

Did the Lord reveal any unclean areas while in the Secret Place? What were my victories over these areas? Have I noticed a difference in my time with the Lord?

_____

_____

_____

Week Twenty-Two ~ Blurred Vision

Can't See the Forest for the Walking Trees

> "... Some people brought [Yeshua] a blind man and begged Yeshua to touch him. Taking the blind man's hand, he led him outside the town. He spit in his eyes, put his hands on him and asked him, 'Do you see anything.' [The man] looked up and said, 'I see people, but they look like walking trees.' Then [Yeshua] put his hands on the blind man's eyes again. [The man] peered intently, and his eyesight was restored so that he could see everything distinctly. Yeshua sent him home with the words, 'Don't go into town.'"
>
> Mark 8:22b-26

Hadass opened the door to her tiny apartment. She kicked off the worn shoes from her sore feet and walked a few steps to the kitchen to plop the heavy grocery sack on the counter.

A weary sigh escaped into the silence as she put away the cans of generic-label soup and store-brand mac and cheese.

She prepared her simple dinner and took it to the living room. Hadass turned on the old television and prepared to eat her meal. The colorful images of wealth and opulence soon turned her plain meal into a tasteless disappointment.

Why wasn't she prospering? Why didn't she have an exciting career when instead she was cleaning offices? Had she offended God in some way so that he wasn't giving her prosperity? Hadass shoved the chipped plate away.

Is our vision blurred by life? Is it difficult to see the blessings God has given us?

This week's passage is an unusual one. Found within what Yeshua did and the blind man's responses are several interesting things that hold practical applications for us.

First, Yeshua led the blind man out of the city. A group of people had brought him to the Messiah for healing (v. 22). Perhaps, Yeshua led him away from the people because they were distracting to the man. Second, Yeshua spat on the man's eyes; he didn't spit into the dirt and rub a poultice of mud. He spat straight onto the guy's eyes. That definitely wasn't what I would have expected or asked for. Was the man embarrassed? I think I would have been.

After all that drama, the result was disappointing. His vision was only partially restored.

The man had three choices: he could have been content with the blurred vision (At least he had some vision, right?); he could have walked away feeling he had had a second-rate miracle and doubting his initial confidence that this Yeshua could do anything; or he could chose to honestly assess his vision, confess it to the Lord, and wait.

Thankfully, he chose the third option.

Yeshua placed his hands on the man again. The verse says the man "peered intently," and then he was able to see "everything distinctly." Finally, Yeshua asked the healed man to not go back into town, but to go home. Why? Was it possible this man needed the solitary focus on the Healer rather than the phenomenon of the healing? Would the crowd turn this miracle into something other than the Messiah's natural, loving act?

Hadass' existence was interrupted by the world's voices. Each day, they presented expectations that confused and discouraged her. After she had shoved away her plate, she walked to the television and shut it off. Hadass picked up her worn Bible and began reading passages of promises from God to her.

As she read, the Lord brought to mind her conversations lately with the owner of the multimillion-dollar company for which she cleaned and how she had offered to pray for him and his family as they struggled through his wife's cancer. The wealthy man's face had changed from despair to hope, as though she had given a priceless jewel to him. He had thanked her with tearful eyes. Hadass continues to lift up prayers for healing—and this family's salvation.

What blessings in our lives are we not seeing clearly? Are we embarrassed by our life? Have the expectations of the world or our own outlook blurred our vision of God's calling for our lives? Are we discontent when we compare our lives with others'—believers or otherwise?

This week, let's focus intently on what God may be showing us. Are we ready to set ourselves apart and allow him to do what he needs to do—even if he needs to spit? Let's be absorbed in thankfulness for his many blessings.

Adonai Kadishkhem (Lord who sets you apart), I'm not quite sure if I understand what the spitting is all about. If I need to understand, I trust that you'll show me because you love me. This week, show me how to intently focus on any areas of blurred vision. Show me how to set myself apart to hear your expectations. I trust you. In Yeshua's Name. Amen

Let's take it to the Secret Place:

Is my vision blurred? If so, in what areas?

_____

_____

_____

_____

Do I listen more to the voices around me (e.g., media or other people) than to the Lord? How has this manifested itself in my life?

_____

_____

List 10 new blessings each day this week.
When was the last time I thanked God for these?

_____

_____

_____

_____

_____

_____

_____

_____

_____

_____

End of Week Twenty-Two:

Did I focus intently on the Lord in the Secret Place? Did I see distinctly the many blessings he has given me? How has this affect my relationship with him?

_____

_____

_____

_____

Week Twenty-Three ~ Dry Eyes

Remember When?

> *"... [A]nd anoint your eyes with eye salve, that you may see."*
> Revelation 3:18b (NKJV)

As much as I hate to admit it, I'm getting older. The adage of wine and cheese tasting better with age is of little consolation. Who wants to be compared to fermented grapes and stinky, moldy cheese?

One of the annoyances of aging is a condition called dry eye. Before anyone suggests to just buy a bottle of eye drops, here's a little biology lesson.

Our tears are comprised of three layers. The mucus layer coats the cornea, so the tear film can adhere to the eye. The middle layer is ninety-eight percent water along with salt, proteins, and other compounds; this provides moisture and supplies oxygen and other important nutrients to the cornea. The outer lipid layer is an oily film that seals the tear film on the eye and helps to prevent the tear's evaporation.

As we age, our bodies produce less oil. If there isn't enough oil, the tears evaporate more quickly, leaving dry areas on the cornea. Blinking can help bring more moisture (as well as clean the eye of impurities), but ultimately, we need the oil to keep the eyes moist.

Are our eyes spiritually dry?

Yeshua is our source of Living Water (John 4:10; John 7:38; Rev. 7:17). When he is in our hearts, he supplies all our needs. He desires to sustain us. We can "drink" from him anytime we want.

Remember when we first accepted Yeshua? How in love we were with him? How on fire we were? We wanted to serve him, give our life for him, and tell the world about him. We had discovered our first love and wanted anyone who would listen to know about it and to experience it for themselves.

Is that fire still in us? That passion?

Like older eyes, have we lost some of the oil that keeps the Living Water from evaporating so quickly from our lives?

The word anoint is derived from the ancient Latin *inunctus*, which means "smear with oil." Has some of our anointing dried up?

"But you have received the Messiah's anointing from HaKodesh (The Holy One), and you know all this ... [T]he Messianic anointing you received from the Father remains in you ... " (1 John 2:20, 27).

The oil is in us, but perhaps we need refreshing of that anointing and renewal of our commitment to the Lord.

Anointing is about consecration: to be set apart and dedicated to God's service and to be imparted with gifts enabling us to advance the Kingdom of God. Do we need to rededicate our lives to God's service? Have we strayed from our original calling to advance God's Kingdom?

This week, let's let the Holy Spirit examine our eyes to see if the oil of his anointing needs refreshing.

Simchati (My Joy), do I have dry eyes? Do I need refreshing and reviving from the anointing oil?

This week, please help me to revisit and remember that joy of my salvation. Please, Lord, renew a right spirit within me (Ps. 51).

This week in our time together, please show me ways to seek your renewing and refreshing at this time in my life. In Yeshua's Name. Amen.

Let's take it to the Secret Place:

What was I like when I first believed in Yeshua as my Messiah? How did I feel? What did I do?

_____

_____

_____

_____

How am I different today? Why?

_____

_____

_____

_____

Begin a list of ways God has begun to refresh and renew me.

_____

_____

_____

_____

_____

_____

_____

_____

Do I still have dry eyes? How was my time remembering my salvation with the Lord in the Secret Place? Is my love for him revived?

_____

_____

_____

_____

Week Twenty-Four ~ Envious Eyes

I Want That?

> *"For where there are jealousy and selfish ambition, there will be disharmony and every foul practice."*
>
> James 3:16

I debated using a parable or someone else's story here, but it didn't seem right to distance myself from this issue as though I haven't battle with this sin. So, here goes my confession, ladies:

I am by nature a very competitive person. Perhaps being the oldest of five children produces this type of personality. I was the firstborn, so why can't I be first at everything?

There is such a thing as healthy competition, but it's also very easy for competition to morph into envy. And this, unfortunately, happens to me a lot.

One of my dearest friends is not a believer. She is, however, one of the wisest women I know. I believe God has given her the gift of a practical understanding of life. And she does this with a great sense of humor.

When we were both pregnant with our first children, I was jealous because her family was close by to celebrate every day and help her through the rough moments. After our babies were born, hers was showered with gifts and love. My husband and I lived several thousand miles away from our family during most of my daughter's life so she seldom experienced the simple joys of being around her grandparents and other family.

My friend didn't want to have more children but became pregnant a few years later. I longed for a second child and yet my womb was shut permanently.

Eventually, my friend had three children and was an amazing mother, who juggled the household demands with grace and style.

I seemed to be in a constant state of angst, wondering if I was the best mother I could be or if my daughter was the best. I tried to impose my competitive mind with its polluted thoughts of envy on my poor daughter.

The envy ate at me. I knew jealousy was sinful, and I knew I was to be a good testimony to my friend, but as the years went by and each month brought another menstrual cycle and no child, I was ashamed and angry.

Ashamed that I wasn't the good testimony I should have been for my friend and angry at God for not blessing me with more children. I fought the jealousy and doubted the goodness of God when he gave children to someone who didn't even believe in him.

The New King James Version of this week's passage says, "For where envy and self-seeking exist, confusion and every evil thing are there." That was how I felt—confused.

At that time, I didn't know how to take the turmoil of hurt and sinful envy to the Secret Place and allow the Lord to help me battle through it. I tried to hide its reprehensible existence until it grew into an ugly monster. I allowed that monster to yank me from the arms of the Lord. For several years, I wanted nothing to do with the Lord. The weird thing was I still believed in him, but I gave him the silent treatment.

Envy robbed me of my relationship with the Lord, and I watched and allowed it to happen.

Thankfully, the Lord pulled me from this pit of putrid gunk, hosed me off, and showed me how I could keep from falling into the cesspool again. (Can you tell that I'm not proud of this period of my life?) He showed me how a heart of gratitude and thanksgiving, despite the lack, battles the strongest temptations of envy.

Today, the punches of envy don't bother me as much; in fact, I feel honest joy and excitement for others most of the time. However, every once in a while, something about their success hits the old wounds, and I'm hurting again. I have to watch I don't develop unhealthy eyes.

This week, join me in watching for those green-with-envy eyes.[1]

Avinu Malkaynu (My Father, my King), I confess that I have envious eyes toward _____. I don't want to. Can you remind me this week of your great love and blessings so I don't have to be jealous of anyone else's blessings? In any case, I choose to renounce and rebuke the jealousy. In Yeshua's Name. I am so grateful of your love. Thank you, Abba. Amen.

Let's take it to the Secret Place:

Where are my most tender spots from the sin envy? Why?

_____

_____

_____

_____

_____

Have I held on to envious eyes? If so, for how long and why?

_____

_____

_____

_____

_____

List some things I'm envious of, and then next to them, list how I can combat this sin with gratitude.

_____

_____

_____

_____

_____

_____

_____

_____

Did I have victory in the Secret Place? How did the Lord help me battle the sin of envy? How has this affected my relationship with him?

_____

_____

_____

_____

Week Twenty-Five ~ Tunnel Vision

Oh, I Didn't See That

> *"We demolish arguments and every arrogance that raises itself up against the knowledge of God; we take every thought captive and make it obey the Messiah."*
>
> 2 Corinthians 10:4b-5

Dana hovered by the window, watching her daughter, Aviva, ride her bicycle around the driveway. Dana's surveillance moved around the perimeters of the dead-end street. First, to the woods—was that movement? Any pervert could hide in the trees, or what if a hunter should miss his target and hit her daughter?

When the mother was certain that no threat lurked in that direction—for now—she moved her inspection to the busy cross street a block up from the house.

Aviva was pretty protected within the confines of their driveway. Still, the dangers of some negligent driver on their cell phone who missed seeing the stop sign and a ten-year-old on her bike were all too real. Dana's body shuddered as the vivid scene played out before her in her mind.

As if reading Dana's thoughts, Aviva's large green eyes looked toward her. Guilt for being so strict with her daughter welled up again, but the mother pushed it down. Protecting her daughter was too important.

The mother looked at her watch, a long list of household chores waited for her. After five more minutes, she would call Aviva in to read a book, watch TV, or something.

Her eyes moved up the empty street.

Dana felt bad that her daughter couldn't freely ride the streets of her neighborhood like her friends. She sighed. Dana remembered feeling the same way when she was growing up; her friends were allowed to walk and ride their bikes all around their small town, but she was restricted—for her own good—to her street. After all, it was possible to be kidnapped twice in a lifetime. Wasn't it?

Dana shivered and then wrapped her arms around herself. She came against a cold that had nothing to do with the weather.

Aviva stopped riding her bike and put her feet back on the ground; she look toward the empty street and then back at her mother. Those beautiful eyes pleaded. Dana shook her head. Aviva bowed her head, then climbed back on her bike, and continued her tight circle within the restrictions of the driveway.

Do our thoughts rise against the knowledge of God? I'm not talking about sexual fantasies or morally inappropriate images (although those would qualify, too). What about imaginations that keep us from living our lives the way God has called us? Fears like Dana's can strangle the vision that God has for both her and her daughter's life.

How about other imaginations like what we would really like to say to our bosses, boyfriends, or husbands? Do we create whole scenarios in our minds to justify not doing tasks to which God has called us? Or remold and manipulate past events in our minds so we don't have to be accountable for them?

These are strongholds in our lives, and we battle them on the largest battlefield—our minds.

This week's passage is taken from a powerful text in 2 Corinthians 10:1–6. Sha'ul (Paul) warns the people of Corinth that there are strongholds in their lives and around them. Our weapons are spiritual, and one of those weapons is to take captive opposing thoughts and submit them to Yeshua.

The Lord spoke to Dana in her Secret Place about her vain imaginations and how they were opposing his authority. It took time, but Dana began recognizing those thoughts for what they were and took control of them. She mentally and verbally bound the thoughts like a prisoner and presented them to Yeshua. The thoughts disappeared in the Messiah's presence like wisps of smoke. The result was new freedoms and peace for both her and Aviva.

This week, let's allow the Holy Spirit to help us identify any vain imaginations or opposing thoughts that may give us tunnel vision. The Lord has a whole world of ministry before us. Let's not miss any of it.

Lord, by your Holy Spirit point out any thoughts that oppose your authority and strangle the vision you have for me. Whether its fear, pride, envy, unforgiveness, or any combination of these sins, please help me identify what these thoughts look and feel like so I can present them as prisoners to Yeshua. I don't want to waste any more time on these thoughts. Thank you for your grace and mercy. I love you so. In Yeshua's Name. Amen.

Let's take it to the Secret Place:

As I read this devotion, did the Holy Spirit reveal some opposing thoughts? If so, what were they?

_____

_____

_____

_____

What is the theme (fear, pride, envy, or unforgiveness) of most of my vain imaginations? Do they have multiple themes? If so, what are they?

_____

_____

_____

_____

List some of my opposing thoughts, and write how God's truth cancels it.

_____

_____

_____

_____

_____

End of Week Twenty-Five:

The last battlefield is the mind. Did I have victory in the Secret Place? Did I begin learning how to take my opposing thoughts captive? How has this affected my relationship with him?

_____

_____

_____

_____

_____

_____

Part Two
The Eyes God Longs For Us To Have

Are you ready to explore God's passion for you personally? Are you ready to see a side of the Lord you may never have seen?

If you've followed these devotions in order (and there's no rule that says you have to), then you probably feel like you've been through the spiritual wringer. All those what-not-to-dos can be arduous, even though they're important to our spiritual growth.

The last five chapters of the book will focus on connecting in deeper intimacy with God in the Secret Place. There's still some soul-searching here, but hopefully, the exploration of learning what pleases God will be exciting and fulfilling.

For me, discovering what God longs for in me has been—and continues to be—a liberating process. I thought I had to act and be a certain type of person, but God just wanted me. Who knew?

My Beloved loves whisking me away with him. It took a little while to figure out what he was doing and why, but with my new understanding, I love it.

The following devotions will hopefully give practical examples and encouragement for you to either find or more fully enjoy your Secret Place.

It is so worth the effort, my sister. Because guess who's waiting there for you.

Chapter Six

Eyes That Recognize God

Imagine you're in a room full of strangers. You're not sure if these people are friends or foes. You try to engage in casual conversation but are distracted by searching the room for one friendly face—someone who knows you.

Out of the corner of your eye, you see someone. You give your full attention to that person. He approaches you with a steady gaze and a look of such love that it makes your heart race. It's him—the love of your life! He's here.

As we begin this chapter, we'll examine the eyes that God wants us to have for him. Let's explore enlightened, victorious, searching, surprised, and knowing eyes.

Week Twenty-Six ~ Enlightened Eyes

Lifting Our Faces to the Son

"But if we are walking in the light, as he is in the light, then we have fellowship with each other, and the blood of his Son Yeshua purifies us from all sin."

1 John 1:7

I've a picture in my mind of my grandmother hanging up sheets on the clothesline. The sun is shining brightly; a gentle breeze lifts and billows the linens like sailboats on a lake. My grandmother pauses, closes her eyes, and lifts her face toward the sun. There's a beautiful expression on her face, a precious mixture of joy, contentment, and communion with the Lord.

If you've read these devotions in order (don't worry, if you haven't), this is the first devotion addressing how we can have the eyes that God longs for us to have and how to deepen our intimacy with him.

Knowing that most of us struggle to have a quiet time, I wondered how we could add more time in his presence. Then, I saw the picture of my grandmother.

Are we ready to look for moments in the Son where we can simply thank him and soak in his presence? Could those little moments of pause really deepen our closeness with him?

A recent study conducted by Dr. Michael F. Holick, a professor of medicine, dermatology, physiology, and biophysics at the Boston University School of Medicine, concluded that brief, unfettered exposure to sunshine or its equivalent several times a week can help ward off some severe diseases like osteoporosis, hypertension, diabetes, multiple sclerosis, rheumatoid arthritis, depression, and cancers of the colon, prostate, and breast.[1]

Is it possible to take one or two brief Son-shine breaks each day? What would be the spiritual benefit? What could these breaks look like?

Sitting in direct sunlight, there is no darkness. Before we begin our interaction with the Lord, wouldn't it be wonderful to sit totally in the Son with no darkness around us?

Pausing moments throughout the day allows Yeshua to shed light on any dark areas that have crept in. Could it also relieve us of some of the burden and stress?

Nonni sat in one long meeting after another. On her desk were piles of work that she couldn't get to because of all the mind-numbing meetings. She noticed her responses toward coworkers were becoming snippy. She wanted to apologize but justified to herself that they should be more patient with her, considering everything on her plate.

As soon as the justification tunneled into her mind, Nonni felt uncomfortable. She didn't like the way it made her feel.

Rather than moving on to the next meeting right away, she excused herself and went to the ladies room.

She took a deep breath and silently prayed, "Lord, show me any darkness."

It didn't take long before the conviction set in. Nonni repented to the Lord and knew her next step was to repent to her coworkers.

The pause and brief time in the Son gave her a respite and the strength to move on to the next stressful task.

Like Nonni, Edna's morning had been one stressful moment after another. Edna heard the crash and waited for the usual shriek. As she ran toward the ruckus, she wondered when—with yet another interruption—she would have time to finish breakfast dishes, so she could prepare dinner for her husband, who would be home in an hour. It seemed all she had done lately was damage control.

She skidded to a stop in the living room. The broken vase—scattered in tiny slivers on the floor—was from her recently deceased great aunt. It had survived for eighty-five years—until now. Somehow her toddler had knocked the beautiful antique off of the highest bookshelf.

Anger pumped into her with every rapid beat of her heart. Edna grabbed the back of her son's shirt as he attempted to escape. She wanted to shake him, to slap his hands, to punish him.

Edna stopped. She took a deep, shaky breath, directed her son to the corner where his timeout chair stood, and made him sit. His indignant cries filled the room.

Rather than cleaning up the splinters of glass, Edna took another deep breath and silently prayed, "Lord, help me to forgive my son for breaking this expensive vase. Show me how to discipline him in accordance with your will."

The young mother's brief moment in the Son helped her stop the escalating anger, so she could properly discipline her child.

A brief pause would have been welcomed for Molly but she didn't have time. Molly was late, really late. She had a houseful of guests coming for Passover dinner, and this was the third grocery store that she had to visit to get all of the ingredients for their first-night meal.[2]

Someone called her name as she loaded her last bag of groceries into the trunk. Molly looked around and saw Julie from her congregation, waving and walking toward her.

"Not now, please," she thought.

Julie hugged Molly and then excitedly shared that her non-believing parents were coming to her Seder. Julie's parents hadn't visited her and her husband's home since the couple had accepted Yeshua.

Molly struggled to not tap her feet impatiently as the minutes and story wore on. She felt the dark cloud of impatience and insensitivity move in.

She took a deep breath and silently repented to the Lord. The negative feelings began dissipating, and a river of compassion trickled in. Molly took Julie's hand and asked if she could pray for her and her family.

Gratitude replaced Molly's irritation and busyness. During the drive home, she shared another visit in the Son when she worshiped and thanked the Lord for allowing her to share that moment with her friend.

Are there moments in our busy days at work where a refreshing Son-break could help us clear the darkness of the stress, challenges, and disagreements by enlightening our eyes to peace and resolutions? Who struggles with the demands of children and running a household? Throw in diarrhea, a bounced check, the broken washer, and a burnt dinner, and we have a day from which even the best executive would run. Could a break in the Son for a few seconds make a difference? We've all felt the frustration when interruptions disrupted our carefully scheduled plans. Are we ready to choose to take moments in the Son to better discern if this is a God disruption?

This week, let's try taking at least one Son-shine break a day to allow the Lord to enlighten our eyes. Like the mother with the apron (week 11), let's practice taking these important breaks with the Lord.

El Yism'kheyni, (God Who Sustains Me), I'm excited and a little nervous. We're going to spend more time together! I'm not quite sure how this is going to work, but I trust you'll point out moments in my day where you are waiting with refreshment, discernment, conviction, forgiveness, and direction. I love you so much. In Yeshua's Name. Amen.

Let's take it to the Secret Place:

Do I believe I need more moments in the Son? If so, what seems to prevent me from doing this?

_____

_____

_____

_____

_____

Am I ready to commit trying one Son-shine break a day this week? If not, why?

_____

_____

_____

_____

Describe my first try. Was it satisfying? Did I want more?

_____

_____

_____

_____

End of Week Twenty-Six:

Was I able to have some days with the Son? Did I notice any changes in my attitude? How has this affected my relationship with the Lord?

_____

_____

_____

_____

Week Twenty-Seven ~ Victorious Eyes

Our Leader Fights with Us

> "I will sing to the LORD, for he has triumphed gloriously! ... [T]he LORD is my strength and song, and he has become my salvation ... The LORD is a man of war; the LORD is his name."
>
> Exodus 15:1–3 (NKJV)

My husband and I love the movie *Independence Day*. This sci-fi film is about aliens from another planet who nearly destroy the population of Earth. A few hundred people, including the president, survive in the United States. A scientist thinks he has discovered a way to defeat the all-powerful enemy, but it will take a diversion for him to complete the task.

Of course, the odds are against them. The diversion consists of a group of nonmilitary pilots who must distract a huge spaceship. I won't spoil the story for those who haven't seen it, but the best scene for me is when the president gives a motivating speech to the nervous pilots, who are ready to possibly meet their doom.

He doesn't sugarcoat the odds, but he inspires them with heartfelt words and then sends the pilots to their planes. Then, the president also suits up, climbs into the cockpit, and flies into battle with the rest of the people.

Imagine flying toward possible death and looking over to see your commander—who doesn't have to be there—flying and fighting alongside you.

That's what our Lord does for us in the Secret Place; he battles alongside us. Although this type of battle is not spiritual warfare per se (though it can come into play), we can battle temptations, emotions, and certain behaviors that cause problems or sin in our lives.

One of the problems Janie struggled with was lying—not big lies, just little exaggerations that sounded like the truth. Like when her boss asked if she had completed her report, she answered that she was almost finished—when she hadn't started. She'd been thinking about the report. That should count, right?

Lately, Janie has felt convicted about lies. Every once in a while, she'd run across a Bible passage that spoke of liars "burning in the lake of fire and brimstone." She'd reason that surely that didn't include her. Then, she wondered why she continued to lie when it was a sin?

Janie's time in the Secret Place became increasingly more strained and not a restful place to which she looked forward.

One day, after feeling the sword of conviction run through her *kishkes* (gut) after another biblical warning against lying, she repented for not caring enough to turn from her sin. She asked the Lord to help her overcome the horrible habit.

Day after day, she battled the temptation to lie. Janie soon became grateful for the conviction she felt after she gave into the temptation because she knew forgiveness would follow her repentance.

Janie's Secret Place was her safe place to discuss openly her problem and also discover the root of why she developed this predilection. God gave her victorious eyes over this temptation.

Like Janie, Betty had a problem that kept rearing its head, and it was taking a toll on her marriage. Betty watched as her husband got into his car and squealed out of the apartment building's parking lot. She worked to control her rapidly beating heart. Part of her wanted to say, "Whatever!" Another part of her wanted to run after him and beg him to stop.

Betty dragged her feet to the bedroom and then threw herself on the bed. The second her face hit the comforter, the tears fell.

"Why?" she thought angrily. "Why do we fight all of the time? Why did I feel it is somehow my fault? How can it be? I am right after all."

And that was the problem. Betty needed to always be right. Betty knew something wasn't working, but she also knew where to take her problem.

She sat up and moved to the floor onto her knees. The tears flooded her face, down her neck, and onto her pajamas.

"Lord, help me! I don't know where to begin. I am right, and my husband doesn't understand. How can we fix this?"

So it wasn't much of a prayer. Yet, Betty was in the best position: on her knees in the Secret Place. Because she understood that the best place to battle the problem was with the Lord, even though she didn't fully comprehend the problem's cause, she stuck it out until she felt a release from the Lord.

The Lord worked side by side with her for months until Betty had an epiphany and began to utilize her spiritually-given fruit of self-control.

I remember in these sort of situations how, after I had to face another round of balagans (chaotic messes) due to my poor decisions, a very wise woman told me, "If you step in a puddle over and over again, it's not the puddle's fault, it's yours."

Are we stepping in puddles that cause us and the people around us stress? Take it to the Secret Place with an open heart and mind. Let the Holy Spirit show us any culpability on our part, and then allow him to patiently, lovingly battle alongside us to have victory.

This week, let's work on our victorious eyes. Our awesome God longs for us to have victory over the temptations, negative emotions, inappropriate behaviors, and sins that keep us from abundant lives. All he needs us to do is suit up and climb into the cockpit. He'll fly with us into battle.

Yariv, (My Defender), thank you for wanting to battle alongside me against my temptations, negative emotions, inappropriate behaviors, and sins. Thank you accepting me for who I am and loving me enough not to leave me there. So I'm a little nervous about opening myself up to you in such an intimate way, but I trust you that you want the best me that I can be. Here I go. In Yeshua's Name. Amen.

Let's take it to the Secret Place:

Am I nervous about opening new areas to the Lord? Why?

_____

_____

_____

_____

Am I a temptation failure or a puddle-stepper? Or both?

_____

_____

_____

_____

With what would I like the Lord to begin? Why?

_____

_____

_____

_____

End of Week Twenty-Seven:

What did the Lord and I battle together this week? Did we have victory, or are we still in the midst of battle? How does it feel having the Lord fighting beside me?

_____

_____

_____

_____

Week Twenty-Eight ~ Searching Eyes

The Doctor Will See You Now, Your Majesty

"... [T]here was a man named Zacchaeus who was a chief tax collector, and he was rich. And he sought to see who [Yeshua] was, but could not because of the crowd, for he was of short stature. So he ran ahead and climbed up into a sycamore tree to see him ... and [Yeshua] said to him, 'Zacchaeus, make haste and come down, for today I must stay at your house ... Today salvation has come to this house, because [Zacchaeus] also is a son of Abraham ....'"

Luke 19:1–10 (NKJV, emphasis mine)

You know those pages and pages of medical forms that you have to fill out when you see a doctor or dentist for the first time? Because of new insurance regulations, I have to fill out a new set every year at my primary physician's office. So as an act of individuality (a.k.a. rebellion) in the midst of bureaucratic conformity, I respond to some of the questions with silly answers.

My favorite question/response is "How would you like to be addressed?" and I've taken to writing, "Your Majesty will do." It's my way of asserting my identity among hundreds of patients. Besides who reads all of those forms?

A few years ago, I searched for a new dentist. After a friend recommended one, I called to schedule an appointment. The receptionist said she would send out a package of forms.

Huh. Not only did I have to complete the lengthy forms, but I had to mail in my paperwork to Dr. Victoria's office a week before my visit.

After I arrived for my first appointment, the receptionist gave me a giggled welcome and then called out, "She's here, Doctor.".

More giggles followed.

The dentist appeared with a wide smile, extended her hand, and said, "It's so good to finally meet you, Your Majesty."

Do we long to be seen in a world where we are just one of the masses? To feel unique and special even though we've done nothing that merits it in the world's eyes? Do we have eyes that search the world for acceptance and recognition?

This week's passage tells Zacchaeus' story. Verse three says, "He sought to see who Yeshua was." Zacchaeus was short and couldn't see above the heads of the crowd, so he humbled himself and, with the enthusiasm of a child, climbed a tree.

The little man was of dubious character. Although he was a wealthy man, he was a tax collector[3]—a traitor to his own people.

We can imagine Zaccheus picked on as a child and perhaps as a young man as well. Maybe his own family didn't think that he'd amount to anything. Clearly, he sought to attain value any way that he could, even at the expense of his people and identity.

But salvation came to Zaccheus the day Yeshua called him from the tree. He repented and in accordance with the Torah[4] committed to making restoration for what he had stolen.

Yeshua not only acknowledges Zaccheus repentance, but calls him a son of Abraham—almost as though Yeshua were giving Zaccheus back his Jewish identity.

Like Zaccheus, Peri had found an identity of her own making that had telling consequences. Peri stepped out of the shower and flinched as she wrapped the towel around her. Although it had been weeks, the bruises still bothered her. But the bruises to her soul went much deeper. Nevertheless, she and the Lord were working on those, too.

At first, Peri couldn't see why the Lord would want to dedicate any effort toward helping her. She'd messed up so badly. Her choice in men—in everything for that matter—had been terrible. She had known better. She had deserved everything that happened to her. She had thought she wasn't worth anyone's trouble.

But a wise friend had helped her see she was so worth it to God. As Peri's body healed, she allowed God to heal her emotionally. He took her on a journey of identifying her unhealthy and sinful behaviors. She repented and received God's forgiveness.

Little by little, Peri is changing her identity from how others view her to how God sees her. Her Secret Place is a place of hope for a future of which she doesn't have to be ashamed.

Do we feel lost and insignificant in the crowd? Do we strive to be what the world thinks as successful? Have the consequences of poor decisions caused us to lose our identity in the Messiah? This week, let's be like Zaccheus who "sought to see" Yeshua. Let's seek our identity in him.

O dear Lord, thank you for seeing me. Sometimes I feel so small and insignificant. Sometimes I feel like such a failure. Sometimes I wonder how you can stand to be near me. Thank you that you see me as your daughter. This week in our Secret Place, help me to seek you. Help me to not strive to impress the world or even you but to find the peace and joy of knowing who I am in the Messiah. In his Name. Amen.

Let's take it to the Secret Place:

Have events and/or decisions I've made formed my identity into someone I don't like? Or is my value inflated and causing me problems? How?

_____

_____

_____

_____

List any revelations the Lord gives me about how he sees me.

_____

_____

_____

End of Week Twenty-Eight:

Was I able to seek Yeshua to discover my true identity? What did I learn? How has this deepened my relationship with the Lord?

_____

_____

_____

_____

Week Twenty-Nine ~ Surprised Eyes

Serendipities in the Secret Place

"One of the Torah-teachers [a scribe] came up and heard [the Sadducees and Yeshua] engaged in this discussion. Seeing that Yeshua answered them well ... The Torah-teacher said to him, 'Well said, Rabbi; you speak the truth ...'"

Mark 12:28–34

My husband and I have been married for more than thirty years. That's a lot of history with plenty of opportunities to get to know one other's quirks and idiosyncrasies. One of the most delightful fruits of being together that long is the serendipitous moments of pure joy and laughter.

The other night, we engaged in our nightly cold war—I like the fan on high (all year long), and he likes it off. I won't bore you with the details, because frankly they wouldn't mean anything to you, but the usual battle ended in one of those serendipities of laughter. We laughed so hard and long that we both saw stars and wondered if we had popped a blood vessel. That, of course, made us laugh harder.

The next day, I tried telling this comical story to someone at work. I received that polite smile and nervous why-does-she-think-this-is-funny-and-does-she-really-expect-me-to-laugh? looks. It dawned on me that this was a moment between my husband and me, borne from years of intimacy and friendship. The experience was so much fun that I still chuckle about it.

Have we ever had moments in our Secret Place where we were surprised with an unexpected moment of complete joy and laughter?

Our passage this week highlights Yeshua's encounter with a *Torah*-teacher (a scribe). The teacher obviously had a great love for God's Word and welcomed new insights into his truths. The man was open to learn. So when Yeshua answered the man's honest questions, he was wonderfully surprised by Yeshua's answers and desirous to engage in further discussion with him.

Are we desirous to engage more deeply with the Lord? How can we have those moments of joyful surprise?

Frieda sat at the breakfast table, eating her granola and blueberries. Her Bible and devotional were next to her as they were every morning for as long as she had been a believer. As a second grade teacher, she needed this quiet time before the usual loud and hectic day with her class.

She took a spoonful of cereal and chewed. Her eyes came across a passage that she'd read many times about David cutting off part of King Saul's robe while Saul was relieving himself (1 Sam. 24). Frieda snickered a little and then remembered an event from her days in grade school. Her friends had dared her to write something on the chalkboard behind the teacher's desk when she had gone to turn in her paper. How nervous and excited Frieda had felt as she had stood behind her teacher and asked a silly question to distract the woman as she had picked up a piece of chalk and scribbled. She only got as far as "Mrs. H—" before her classmates' titters had given her away. The look on her teacher's face …

The similarities of the biblical story and her own threw Frieda into a bout of laughter. Unfortunately, she still had a mouth full of fruit and granola, which shot out of her mouth and onto the pristine pages of her Bible.

Her hilarity grew as she sopped up the mess. The irony that she now had a classroom of mischievous students wasn't lost on her. Frieda was put into the little shoes of those precious children that morning. The surprise caused Frieda to look up to the Lord in gratitude for the joyful refreshment.

Today, when Frieda happens on that crinkled and blueberry-stained page of her Bible, she still laughs in delight. She's reminded of that moment of joy, refreshment, and revelation.

Wouldn't it be great to plan moments such as these in our Secret Place? Regrettably, that's not how it works. However, as we deepen our relationship with the Lord, we can expect these unexpected joyful occasions. They're God's hugs and kisses.

This week, let's prepare our hearts for the surprises. Who knows when and how they will appear—and isn't that half of the fun?

Simchati, (My Joy), I'm excited! My Secret Place with you can be fun, too? I'm ready. There's laughter already bubbling in my spirit. This week, could you give me one of those moments? I love you! In Yeshua's Name. Amen.

Let's take it to the Secret Place:

Have I ever had a serendipity of laughter with the Lord in our Secret Place? If so, please describe it.

_____

_____

_____

_____

_____

Is it possible for me to "prepare" for a surprise? If so, how?

_____

_____

_____

_____

Have I ever been surprised by how well God knows me? If so, please describe.

_____

_____

_____

_____

_____

End of Week Twenty-Nine:

Did the Lord give me surprised eyes this week? What did I learn? How did it deepen my relationship with him?

_____

_____

_____

_____

Seeing Before We See

> *"Yeshua heard that they had thrown the man out. He found him and said, 'Do you trust in the 'Son of Man?' 'Sir,' he answered, 'tell me who he is, so that I can trust in him. Yeshua said to him, 'You have seen him. In fact, he's the one speaking with you now.' 'LORD, I trust!' he said, and he kneeled down in front of him."*
>
> *John 9:35–38*

They say everyone has a twin somewhere in the world—a look-alike. Heddie and Talya didn't have to look any further than their own workplace to find theirs.

Heddie had worked in her family's business for most of her adult life. Her name and reputation were well known. Talya had only been with the company for a few years, so most often, it was Talya who was mistaken for Heddie.

The two women began traveling together for meetings with business associates who knew Heddie but hadn't seen her recently. The incidences of mistaken identity were most embarrassing for those who at one time considered themselves Heddie's dear friends but ended up chatting with a stranger.

The awkward scenarios typically began, "Remember when we—" Talya always cringed with the inevitable embarrassment that was about to occur.

Over the years, Talya learned diplomatic and gracious interruptions to prevent the person from being too embarrassed, but it was hard to miss the disappointment and shock on their faces.

Do we confuse Yeshua's identity with our own concept of who he is? Is this because we don't know him as well as we thought or because we haven't spent as much time with him as we should?

The passage in John 9 is the story of the blind man who Yeshua healed by rubbing mud on the man's eyes and then instructing him to wash it off. After the man washed his eyes, his sight was restored.

The Pharisees then threw the newly healed man into an intense investigation. This story is one of my favorites because the angry accusations didn't rob him of the awe and wonder of his healing. In fact, the more they interrogated him, the more he came to an understanding of who Yeshua was.

Although others in the community came to believe in the Messiah because of what they saw, this man knew before he saw—before he met Yeshua in person.

Are we getting to know Yeshua in our Secret Place? Are we practicing awe and knowing even in the midst of persecution (Ps. 119:161)?

Aliza was a new believer. She came from an Orthodox Jewish background and found great joy in the freedom of Yeshua's salvation and forgiveness. She loved the Messianic community, but had to get used to having interactions with Christians, who shared her Messiah, because mostly her childhood encounters with people who called themselves Christians weren't pleasant.

Still, the young woman loved sharing her faith with other believers. That's why when the nicely dressed people had come to her door to share their faith, she had invited them in. But a little while into the discussion, Aliza's stomach bothered her and her heart began racing. She felt a cloud of confusion settle over her—the Jesus who these nice people were talking about didn't seem to be the same Yeshua in whom she believed.

When she questioned their theology, the once-polite people became more forceful. She sensed a familiar threat. Aliza wanted these people out of her home, now!

Once the missionaries were shown the door, Aliza took her confusion to the Lord. She was able to battle several of the thoughts with what she knew in the Bible. The next day, she took her concerns to the rabbi's wife. The rabbi's wife explained that those people weren't true believers and then gave Aliza scriptural defenses to the false doctrine.

Although disconcerting, Aliza thanked the Lord for the incident. Not only was it her first practical lesson in discernment, but it initiated a drive to truly know Yeshua, so she could easily recognize him from the false messiahs the enemy might bring her way.

Have we mistaken a messiah that is not Yeshua? Are we ready to train our eyes to know him in accordance with Scripture? Are our discernment muscles exercised and ready to sense false doctrine?

This week, let's work on our knowing eyes that can recognize Yeshua from imposters—even our own false assumptions that we may have about him

Ruach Ha'Emet, (Spirit of Truth), this is very serious. I want to know you. Reveal any false identities that I may have about you or Yeshua. Help me to exercise my discernment muscle. In Yeshua's Name. Amen.

Let's take it to the Secret Place:

Have I ever been confused by a misunderstanding of who the Lord is (e.g., God would never allow bad things to happen to me)? If so, describe it. How did I battle this confusion?

_____

_____

_____

_____

_____

Am I willing to look more closely to see if I have mistaken the Lord for someone else? How can I defend myself against false teachings?

_____

_____

_____

_____

How will I exercise my discernment muscles this week?

_____

_____

_____

_____

End of Week Thirty:

Did the Lord reveal any areas where I've mistaken his identity? How did he reveal more of himself to me this week? How has it deepened my relationship with him?

_____

_____

_____

_____

Chapter Seven

Understanding Eyes

*W*e've all had those aha! moments, when the emotional or spiritual switch flips on, illuminating some mystery or struggle that has plagued us. Situations, motives, and emotions resonate with clarity when we finally understand what God has been trying to tell us.

Over the next five weeks, we'll search for observant, watchful, perceptive, acknowledging, and comprehending eyes. The Lord longs for us to see the messes, misguided direction, truth, the opportunities for praise, and the ways to grow in our faith.

And maybe along the way, we will be able to share those revelations with others who struggle with the same issues.

Week Thirty-One ~ Observant Eyes

Eww! Is That Mine?

> "For seven days you are to eat matzah [unleavened bread]——on the first day remove the leaven from your houses."
>
> Exodus 12:15a

> "... Don't you know the saying, 'It takes only a little hametz [leaven] to leaven a whole batch of dough.'? Get rid of the old hametz, so that you can be a new batch of dough, because in reality you are unleavened. For our Pesach [Passover] lamb, the Messiah, has been sacrificed."
>
> I Corinthians 5:6—7

Kayla stood with a broom, rag, and a bottle of furniture polish. Passover was just a few days away, and her mother had a cleaning list as long as War and Peace. Most of her Christian friends' mothers had also drafted them into spring-cleaning this week. If they had known the Jewish people were responsible for bringing this drudgery into the world, they'd probably never speak to her again.

Her chore today was giving the living room a thorough cleaning. Kayla looked at her grime-fighting weapons and the room before her. She shook her head. Her mother was such a neat freak that Kayla would have been shocked to find a speck of dust anywhere.

The teenager began by dusting and polishing the furniture and then finished by sweeping the floors.

"Cool!" she thought. "That didn't take long."

Kayla grabbed the phone to call one of her girlfriends. It looked like she could make it to the mall after all.

"Kayla?" Kayla recognized her mother's disapproving tone. "There's no way that you finished this room."

Kayla continued dialing. "Muh—ther. Look for yourself. It's perfect."

Her mother took the phone and disconnected the call.

"Dear, there's no way you thoroughly cleaned this room."

She took her daughter's hand and walked her toward the wall of bookcases. The teenager rolled her eyes.

"Here, Kayla," her mother rubbed her finger across a row of books and then presented the dirty evidence. "There's dust on all of these books. Did you remove them and polish the shelves?"

"You're kidding, right?" Kayla's fists went to her hips. "No one sees that. Who would ever know?" Her mother gave her the I-would-know look.

For what seemed like an eternity, Kayla's mother guided her to all of the dust and dirt hideouts. Begrudgingly, Kayla was impressed that her mother was able to search out the grime that she'd completely missed. Her eyes were opened to the filth that she had overlooked.

Do we search for the "dirt" inside our hearts? Or have we overlooked hidden messes?

Our passages this week speak about the physical and spiritual preparation for Passover and the Feast of Unleavened Bread. As the Messianic and non-Messianic Jewish communities prepare for Passover, we clean out any foods with leaven in it.

Although it may seem pretty straightforward to remove cans and packages of yeast and our loaves of bread, in today's world yeast is everywhere. By reading the labels of most prepared foods, you'll find the ingredients contain yeast products. Then, there's baking soda, baking powder, most wines, and all beers, packaged cookies, and crackers. It takes an experienced eye to catch all of the hiding places for leaven.

As the New Covenant passage illustrates, all it takes is a little leaven (sin) to leaven the whole lump of dough (us).

This week, let's do some spiritual spring-cleaning in preparation for our spiritual Passover. Let's allow the Holy Spirit to guide us to areas in our lives that have hidden sins. Once our eyes are opened to the spiritual messes, we have the Lord's promise that he'll help us clean up.

El Ro'i, (God Who Sees), it doesn't matter if this is the appointed season for Passover or not, I commit this week to doing some spiritual housecleaning. By your Ruach HaKodesh (Holy Spirit) guide me to any hidden leaven that could cause further damage in my life and in our relationship. Thank you for your Passover Lamb, Yeshua, whose blood makes atonement for my sin. In honor of his redeeming work and love. Amen.

Let's take it to the Secret Place:

When was the last time I did a serious spring-cleaning of my heart?

_____

_____

_____

_____

Am I willing to allow the Holy Spirit to guide me to places that I've overlooked? Why?

_____

_____

_____

_____

Do I have a plan for cleaning out the spiritual messes? If so, what is it?

_____

_____

_____

End of Week Thirty-One:

What leaven did the Lord reveal to me this week? How did it deepen my relationship with him?

_____

_____

_____

_____

Take a Right, No, Make That a Left

> *"Of the descendants of Yissakhar [Issachar] [there were] men who understood the times and knew what Isra'el ought to do . . ."*
>
> *I Chronicles 12:32*

There's a commercial where a nice-looking fellow in an expensive car is listening to the sensual voice of his navigational system. The man smoothly executes his right turns and left turns. He's in the groove of the step-by-step instructions of the sophisticated system, until—bam!—he crashes through the front window of a restaurant. He was so busy following directions that he wasn't watching where he was going.

Are we listening to the world's guidance system and not watching where God wants us to go?

The message of this week's passage is easy to miss. Just a few words, "the sons of Issachar who had understanding of the times, to know what Israel ought to do," yet their significance, especially for us as we train our eyes to be watchful, is worthy of meditation.

Sadie had *schpilkis* (ants in her pants, edgy). Questions and thoughts about her boyfriend consumed her. "Is he the one? Will he ever propose? Should I just move on? What should I do?"

The nervous woman went from friend to friend asking for prayer. There were several women in her congregation with gifts of discernment, and Sadie got in touch with them to get a clear word from the Lord.

There was one woman in particular, Joan, from whom Sadie had wanted prayer but they had been missing one another. The last couple days, Joan hadn't even returned her messages. Then, someone told her that Joan had had the flu. After another week, Sadie was desperate to hear from the Lord. She couldn't wait for services so she could get more prayer.

Sadie finally spied Joan and her family as they entered the synagogue after services had started. Sadie couldn't concentrate because her anticipation roiled in her stomach like a dogfight.

The Aaronic benediction was barely out of the rabbi's mouth when Sadie jumped from her seat and made a beeline toward Joan.

Sadie breathlessly re-explained her dilemma and grabbed the woman's hand. Joan withdrew her hand then turned her head to cough a few times. She smiled at Sadie.

"Sadie, I have been praying for you since your first message." Joan took a tissue from her purse and placed it to her nose. "And I do sense the Lord has given me something to tell you. Hold on, I'm going to sneeze."

The young woman could barely contain herself waiting as Joan sneezed several times then blew her nose.

"What is the Lord going to tell me? What does he want me to do?" At last she was going to hear from him!

"I'm sorry, dear," said the woman who held Sadie's future in her hands—hands that placed the soiled tissues back in her purse. "I believe what the Lord said was, 'Sadie, why are you asking everyone but me? Don't be an eavesdropper of my word.'"

"What?"

The woman smiled and wrapped her arm around Sadie's waist.

"Sadie, have you asked the Lord what you should do?"

Sadie felt a rush of heat on her face.

"Of course, I've asked him. Thousands of times."

"But have you listened? Waited for his answer?"

Sadie knew she hadn't really waited. She had wanted a quick answer and figured enlisting other prayers meant a quicker response.

The wise woman had prayed for Sadie to be able to watch and listen for God's answer. Joan offered to continue praying for Sadie, and when Sadie heard from the Lord, Joan would be happy to pray for confirmation and wisdom in what to do next.

Are we eavesdroppers of God's Word? Do others have to spoon-feed us or are we able to dine with the Lord ourselves? Do we train our eyes to be watchful for understanding in these times so we know what to do?

This week, let's take another step in our relationship with the Lord and see if our guidance system is the world's, other believers', or God's.

El Elyon, (God Most High), I think I may need an adjustment in my guidance system. This week, please show me if I'm using the world's system, other believers' systems, or even my own when I should be using yours. I don't want to be an eavesdropper and not really understand what's going on around me. I want to be more in tune with you and what you're doing in my life and around me. Help me to have watchful eyes fixed on you for my direction. Thanks for your gracious patience. I love you. In Yeshua's Name. Amen.

Let's take it to the Secret Place:

Whose guidance system am I using?
How does this generally play out in my life?

_____

_____

_____

Am I an eavesdropper of God's Word? Do I seek the answers to my questions from God or others? Why?

_____

_____

_____

Do I have watchful eyes so that I have an understanding of what happens in my life and around me? Why or why not?

_____

_____

_____

End of Week Thirty-Two:

Are my eyes more watchful? Did I begin training myself to go straight to the Lord for guidance? How has it deepened my relationship with him?

_____

_____

_____

_____

Week Thirty-Three ~ Perceptive Eyes

Accurate May Not Be Truth

> *"My mind and body may fail; but God is the rock for my mind and my portion forever." .*
>
> Psalms 73:26

Glenda Watson Hyatt was born with cerebral palsy. Doctors recommended to her parents that Glenda be institutionalized because they said she wasn't able to communicate well enough to be understood or use her hands to take care of herself. They believed that she had little hope for a meaningful life. This Canadian family chose to ignore the medical advice. Although the doctors' perceptions about Glenda's verbal skills and use of her hands were accurate, their understanding of those limitations on her life was far from true.

Today, Glenda is married, a published author[1] (which she typed with her left thumb), an international speaker, and an award-winning equestrienne. Glenda understands her handicap, but she chose *God's perception* of her potential.

Do we allow challenges and discouraging remarks to keep us from all that God has for us?

"You'll never amount to anything, Livia. Forget about college."

Livia tried to keep her classmates' hurtful remarks from penetrating the protective shield she had fashioned after years of these barbs, but it wasn't working.

It was official. She *was* stupid. Her first test in high school had proved it. She had so wanted to make a fresh start at her new school. She had studied hard for the history exam. Her mom had helped her memorize dozens of facts and dates. But as soon as she had read the test questions, she had gotten confused, as though she hadn't known anything at all.

As Livia walked home her thoughts fed the feelings of failure. Did God hate her or something? She thought their relationship was real. Was she fooling herself with him, too? Maybe because she couldn't read her Bible like everyone else he was punishing her.

She walked into the kitchen, dragging her backpack on the floor.

Her mother turned from the stove and smiled, but the smile turned to concern.

"Liv, what happened? Why aren't you at ballet class?"

"I got a D." The dejected teenager flopped onto a chair and released the tears that she'd bravely kept in. "I'm stupid. Just stupid!"

Livia's mother raced to her daughter's side.

"No, you are not stupid." She wrapped her arms around Livia. "I don't understand. You studied so hard. You knew the material backward and forward."

"It's because I'm stupid, Mom. It's time to deal with this."

Her mother shushed her.

"Yes, it is time to deal with it. Let's pray."

The mother and daughter prayed, cried, and then prayed some more.

That weekend, Livia was alone listening to praise and worship in the living room. She closed her eyes and began dancing. This was something she knew—she wasn't stupid when she danced; she was free. It was her offering to the Lord.

A few steps into the song, something happened. It was as though the music entered her body and turned it into praise. Her heart poured out her love for the Lord into her limbs. Livia was lost in worship that was both joyful and bittersweet.

As the song ended, Livia lifted her hands and face upward. She felt as much as heard the words, "*My* strength is made perfect in your weakness." She wrapped her arms around herself like a hug and released a contented sigh.

Livia opened her eyes to see her family standing and watching her. Their faces bathed in tears.

Several weeks later, Livia's mother read an article about dyslexia. The symptoms were strikingly similar to Liv's challenges. Livia was tested and diagnosed with the learning disorder. She now receives special tutoring.

Although she has to work harder than her friends to do the simplest reading exercises, she doesn't care because God's strength is made perfect in her weakness (2 Cor. 12:9)—a passage, which, by the way, she loves reading in her Bible.

Are there physical or emotional challenges that keep us from the abundant life God has for us? Can we understand our weak areas but not allow them to impede our relationship or walk with the Lord?

This week, let's ask the Lord for perceptive eyes that have insight into any emotional and/or physical challenges we might have. Are we ready to seek God's perceptions of our limitations and not be constrained by the world's expectations?

Abba, your strength is made perfect in my weakness—and I'm weak because _____. *With you by my side, I can overcome and work through, in, or around my challenges. It's your perception I seek, LORD. I praise you in these weaknesses. In Yeshua's Name. Amen.*

Let's take it to the Secret Place:

Do I have any physical and/or emotional handicaps? If so, how has it impacted my life?

_____

_____

_____

What has been my perception of these challenges in my life? Why?

_____

_____

_____

As I have sought the Lord, has he shown me a different perception of my disabilities? If so, what has he shown me?

_____

_____

_____

End of Week Thirty-Three:

Has my perception of my disabilities changed this week? If so, how? Has it changed the way I relate to the Lord

_____

_____

_____

_____

Week Thirty-Four ~ Acknowledging Eyes

Home Is Where the Heart Is

> "One of [the lepers], as soon as he noticed that he had been healed, returned shouting praises to God, and fell on his face at Yeshua's feet to thank him ... Yeshua said, 'Weren't ten cleansed? Where are the other nine?'"
>
> Luke 17:15–18

Home.

For most of us home represents love, safety, and comfort—our sanctuary. Growing up do you remember...

- ✡ Running home to get money for the ice cream man?
- ✡ Limping home after falling off your bike?
- ✡ Skipping home with a bunch of dandelions in dirty fists?
- ✡ Walking home when you ran out of gas?
- ✡ Calling home because you were afraid?
- ✡ Dragging yourself home when you failed?
- ✡ Returning home for comfort?

It's easy to think of God as our home—our sanctuary. We can run to him anytime that we have a problem or need his intervention. But are our feet as swift to run to him with gratitude and thanksgiving?

This week's passage is simple and powerful. Ten lepers were healed, but only one returned. There's no question all of the men were grateful—they probably shouted their praises to God—but only one returned to the source of their healing, Yeshua.

Marni, fresh from graduate school, began her job as an account executive for a large corporation. She was grateful to the Lord for this opportunity and longed to be a visible witness to those around her.

However, Marni couldn't count the number of times that someone had taken credit for her ideas and the accounts and new clients had gone to her coworkers.

When this happened, the young executive retreated to her cubicle and submitted her feelings of frustration, rejection, and anger to the Lord. She forgave her associates and did her best to walk in that forgiveness. Marni knew that she was in a battle to maintain her integrity in that environment.

Another opportunity to land a major client was presented to her. Marni worked harder and wiser. When her boss called her into his office, she prepared herself for the usual letdown.

She hadn't prepared for success. As her boss relayed the good news—not only did she land the account, but it was the company's largest one—Marni's brain turned to mush. When her boss gave her a raise—and one of the real offices with walls, windows, and a door—her knees knocked like a bad car engine. Somehow she managed a shaky thank you and handshake and then willed her wobbly legs to walk out the door.

Once she was out of earshot, Marni squeaked out, "Thanks, Lord."

The adrenaline rush began in her feet. She did a quick tap dance and then ran down the hall. As she whizzed past the other cubicles, the names of people whom she needed to call lined up in her head. Marni had to make travel arrangements to meet with the client tomorrow and call the art department and media and—

Marni sat in her cubicle and entered all of the to-do items into her electronic organizer while they were fresh in her mind. She picked up her phone and called her parents, her best friend, and the members of her Bible study group and then booked her flight and hotel.

After work, she shopped for some new clothes and luggage and then picked up a burger and chocolate shake. As she filled her tub to take a nice, long bubble bath, she imagined how professional she would look in her new suit and—

"Oh my, I forgot to call my favorite teacher!" she thought.

Marni, when are you going to call me?

She turned off the water.

"Lord? Didn't I thank *you*?"

Not really, she realized. It was just a short breath of thanks before she set about making plans. Marni fell to her knees. It had been hours since God had given her such favor and blessing. She'd had time to shop and talk to just about everyone she knew, but she hadn't spent more than a few seconds of her time thanking him. How readily she had spent time with the Lord when she needed his comfort and wisdom and how quickly had she shoved him into the background when success came. The revelation shocked and frightened her.

Years later, Marni is as careful with her praise and prayers as she is at her job. Whether in her corner office, a taxi, a plane, a hotel room, or her house, she always runs home to her Abba.

Do we invest the same energy in thanksgiving as we do in intercession? This week, let's examine our hearts for acknowledging eyes.

*El Elyon, (God Most High), did I thank you for _____?
I don't want to come to you with just my problems, but I want to invest the same energy in praising you for the many blessings and successes that you have given me. I want to be the one who returns and glorifies you. I want my heart to be your home. In Yeshua's Name. Amen.*

Let's take it to the Secret Place:

Do I consider my earthly home a sanctuary? How has this affected my understanding of God as my home?

_____

_____

_____

Is my heart truly God's home—does he live or visit there?

_____

_____

_____

Am I spiritually prepared for success? Is my investment in praise and gratitude the same as my prayers for needs and wants? Why?

_____

_____

_____

End of Week Thirty-Four:

Did the Lord show me how to have acknowledging eyes? How do I think it will change the way I relate to the Lord?

_____

_____

_____

_____

Sometimes It's the Little Things

> *"The ear that hears the rebukes of life will abide among the wise."*
>
> Proverbs 15:31 (NKJV)

My friend leaned toward me. "We're always working out some flaw in our lives, aren't we? And then, we're always driven to share the revelations with others." I nodded. Boy, was she right.

Sitting together during a grand bat mitzvah reception, she and I were discussing recent breakthroughs that we had experienced. A wonderful party was going on around us, and we had our heads together talking about how God had shown us the darkness in our lives and how to overcome it. Was this just navel-gazing?

Finally, we shrugged and figured, that it was just who we were. What choice did we have—it was probably one of those little personality quirks.

Months later, imagine my surprise when, as I was reading this week's passage, I realized that this wasn't a quirk but a gift. Do we hear the rebukes of life so our eyes comprehend stumbling blocks to our relationship with the Lord?

My Utmost for His Highest says, "The author who benefits you most is not the one who tells you something you did not know before, but the one who gives expression to the truth that has been dumbly struggling in you for utterance."[2]

Have we gained a victory that could help someone else? Do we see the lessons that God puts into our lives and put them to good use? Do we recognize him at work and point him out to others?

From the corner of her eye, Gaby watched her niece Nina playing in her playpen. Gaby's sister and brother-in-law were on a "date," and she'd agreed to baby-sit. She aimlessly flipped through channels with the remote, wondering how early she could put Nina to bed.

A whomph! drew Gaby's attention back to the toddler. The kid had fallen again. Gaby chuckled as her niece's legs and arms moved like windmills as she tried to right herself. Grunting, Nina managed to pull herself up by pinching her little fingers into the mesh walls of the playpen. She held onto the padded railing, squealing with delight, and walked around, pushing toys with her feet. With her tongue sticking out, Nina released the edge and took a step. On her second step, she wobbled and then tumbled onto the soft floor of her playpen.

Gaby switched off the television and walked over to Nina. The little one flopped to her back and then gave her aunt a wet smile. Nina stretched out her arms toward Gaby, who scooped up the wiggly bundle as the two of them giggled.

For nearly an hour, Gaby watched with admiration as Nina attempted to walk. She couldn't count the number of times her niece plopped on her diapered behind, but by bedtime, she'd taken five steps on her own.

The experience brought up emotions Gaby didn't quite comprehend. If someone had told her earlier how much she'd enjoy watching Nina try to walk—even more than the show she had planned to watch—she would have called that person crazy. But there was something else.

When her sister and husband returned home, Gaby told them Nina had taken five steps. The parents were happy, yet clearly disappointed that they had missed the event.

Later when Gaby climbed into bed and snuggled into her comforter, the joy she had felt watching Nina returned. She said her prayers and thanked God for letting her watch her niece. The mental movie of her niece's attempts to walk played and replayed in her head, as though she had missed something.

"Wait a minute, Lord. Is this how you are with me? So you don't get mad at me when I don't do things perfectly? Are you really proud of me for trying? And trying again?" Tears rolled down her cheeks.

Gaby's relationship with the Lord changed that night. She no longer viewed him as watching to make sure she did everything right. She saw him as her loving Daddy who watched her as she tried—and sometimes failed—in her walk. She knew he loved her determination; she knew he loved her.

This reality is so established in Gaby that she loves sharing this story with others who beat themselves up when they fail.

Do we miss unique lessons and messages that God has for us every day? This week, let's open our eyes to any rebukes or lessons that God may be showing us, take them to our Secret Place, and allow him to incorporate them into our spirits. Who knows when our story will bring blessing to someone else?

Abba, train my eyes to comprehend the beautiful, unique, and thought-worthy lessons that you tuck into my life every day; whether they are rebukes to make me wiser or events that help me better understand your character. Be my teacher all day long and not just in our Secret Place. In Yeshua's Name. Amen.

Let's take it to the Secret Place:

Have I ever noticed the rebukes of life? If so, give an example.

_____

_____

_____

Have I ever noticed the examples of God's loving nature in simple events of the day? If so, give an example.

_____

_____

_____

Do I share victories or moments of God's revelation to others who may be struggling with similar problems? If so, give an example.

_____

_____

_____

End of Week Thirty-Five:

Did I begin training my eyes to comprehend the rebukes and lessons that God gives me? How did this play out in our Secret Place?

_____

_____

_____

_____

_____

Chapter Eight

Adoring Eyes

*E*ver been to a spa? Or taken a long relaxing bath?

Adoration is a lot like that—no agendas, goals, or schedules; it is simply focusing on the object of your affection.

Over the next five weeks, we'll search for calm eyes, eyes that dance with delight, eyes that are loving, eyes that give off a beautiful fragrance, and eyes of awe. Hopefully, we'll learn how to more deeply soak in the presence of God, even in the midst of trials and tribulations.

When Moses left the Tent of Meeting, he radiated the presence of God. When we've left our Tent of Meeting, will we too radiate his presence? Will our spiritual spa-time in the fragrance of Yeshua produce an aroma that is pleasing to God?

The Honeymoon Experiment

> "Be still and know that I am God ..."
>
> Psalm 46:10 (NKJV)

Returning from a long month on the road, the singer walked into her beautifully designed apartment. She dropped her luggage and her guitar case on the floor. The instrument released a sad, disconnected tone—like her heart.

She rubbed her eyes still seeing the auditoriums filled with adulation. She wondered how much was for God and how much for her. Although honored that her songs were at the top of charts, did they honor her Creator? Lately, it had bothered her how people longed to touch her as if she were an unfettered conduit to God.

How surprised these fans would be if they knew how empty and frightened she was. How disappointed they would be to know that the passion the singer once felt for the Lord seemed a distant dream.

The sounds of exaltation and success had drowned out the still small voice of her Beloved. She no longer heard his songs of love to her. The deep well of love and peace was dry. Her prayers sounded trite in her own ears. What must they sound like to her Abba? She was desperate for his voice and for the quiet cloak of his presence.

A rumble pushed up from her *kishkes* (gut) and twisted itself into a wail. She slumped to the floor and keened like a wounded animal. The singer lay on the floor a long time, and then softly and tenderly, she heard it. Let go.

Several weeks later, the singer stood with her guitar, Bible, and journal in a near empty apartment. Only a mattress and a chair remained. No television, praise and worship music, or other books.

Her management team had tried to talk her out of this experiment. They told her taking a leave of absence at this point in her career was not wise.

But the singer needed a fast from fame and the creative striving for another song. She craved God's presence, not his inspiration to lead others in praise and worship.

Have we taken a chance on adoration? Do we need to take a fast from distractions that keep us from hearing the Lord?

The Hebrew word for still as used in the above Scripture is *rafa*, which means, "to slacken," or let go.

Even Shabbat, which is meant as a rest and refreshing, can be busy with preparations: getting kids dressed for services, teaching Shabbat School, and the list goes on. Some weeks, it hardly feels restful.

Can we slacken the hold that we have on things, tasks, and even recreation for just a short time? Can we fast from the things that distract us from worship?

The singer lived simply and quietly for one month. It took some time to adjust to the new rhythm and to clear the sound of applause and admiration from her mind. Sometimes her days were spent in study and prayer, sometimes in praise and worship, and other times in silence. Some days, she filled pages in her journal. In time, the singer's heart swelled with recognition when the Lord took his proper place there once again.

It was a bittersweet moment when the fast ended. Like a bride coming back from her honeymoon, she didn't want it to end, but she was eager to resume her life. The singer was ready to return to the ministry to which God had called her, but she never wanted to lose her closeness with him.

This week, let's try our own fast. Can we fast from long conversations on the phone, sleeping in, shopping, the Internet, television, and reading novels and instead spend those moments in stillness? I'm certain the Lord is anxiously waiting to show us how we can if we ask him.

Adon HaShabbat, (LORD of the Sabbath), I need to slacken my hold of things that aren't necessarily bad but sometimes keep me from spending time with you. Show me what I can fast from this week so that you and I can connect at a deeper level. Like a bride waiting to go on her honeymoon with her groom, I'm anxiously longing to hear from you. In Yeshua's Name. Amen.

Let's take it to the Secret Place:

Is there something that I can fast from this week? If so, what?

_____

_____

Planning my honeymoon experiment:

    ✡ When will I go?
    ✡ Where will I go?
    ✡ What will I do?
    ✡ What will I pack?

_____

_____

_____

_____

_____

_____

_____

_____

End of Week Thirty-Six:

How was my honeymoon experiment? Did the Lord and I connect in deeper ways? If so, how?

_____

_____

_____

_____

Week Thirty-Seven ~ Dancing Eyes

Shall We Dance?

> *"Let Isra'el rejoice in their maker, let Tziyon's [Zion's] children take joy in their king. Let them praise his name with dancing ..."*
>
> Psalm 149:2-3a

From the time Maggie was a little girl, she loved to dance. But her strict religious home frowned on any dance other than "dancing in the Spirit." Maggie's longing was limited to her bedroom, where she donned a frilly white petticoat over her clothing and then twirled and tip-toed like a ballerina. As a young woman, Maggie endured a series of thorny affairs with men. She took her unfilled longing for love and excitement, donned clothing to fit the different themes of various bars that she frequented, and then danced to lose herself in the beat of the world's music.

Eventually, Maggie's deepest longing was fulfilled when she accepted Yeshua as her Messiah. He began a gradual process of liberation from her past hurts and helped her overcome her guilt from past sins. The freedom and joy that she felt made her want to dance, but a foot condition now caused her great pain. No medication or therapies eased the hurting.

Maggie joined the music ministry of her congregation and loved to worship the Lord with music, but the longing to worship him with others in Davidic[1] dance only grew.

A rabbi visited and spoke at her congregation. He spoke of God's healing for his children. He offered to pray for anyone wanting healing. Maggie longed to go forward, but she was afraid that she wasn't worthy of healing. Instead, she praised the Lord and reached out to him. A warm sensation began at her feet and traveled up her legs. She felt a strange stretching and then realized her feet no longer hurt. Maggie jumped up and down rejoicing—there was no pain!

A circle of Davidic worshipers formed. Maggie ran forward and joined them—her longing fulfilled.

Do we have longings that we've tried to fulfill on our own? Are there ways that we would like to worship the Lord but are unable to?

Dodi's first visit to the Messianic synagogue was awe-inspiring. She had been a believer for nearly forty years, but she had never seen such joy in worship as when she watched the Davidic worshipers. She ached to join them. But when Dodi shared her experience with the women of her Bible study, they were very put off. Men and women dancing together? Worship was supposed to be dignified and respectful and not a distracting emotional display.

Dodi esteemed these women's opinions greatly, but somehow this one seemed wrong. She decided to go directly to the Lord for his counsel. Did he enjoy this type of praise and worship? Was it meaningful to him? Pouring over her Bible, Dodi found many passages where people danced before the Lord in worship and praise. As she prayed, the Lord brought to mind a childhood memory.

Dodi had wanted a bicycle for her birthday, but it was the Great Depression and money was tight. She had worked hard to suppress her expectations, so when her daddy rolled the shiny refurbished bicycle onto the sidewalk, Dodi screamed and ran to him. She hugged and kissed him with gratitude and then proceeded to dance for joy. "Thank you, Daddy! Thank you! Thank you! Thank you!"

Dodi laughed at the memory and her childlike exuberance. But then she remembered the look on her father's face. The joy he felt because he was able to give his daughter her heart's desire. The happiness he felt at her energetic gratitude. God loved this type of praise and worship, too. There was no doubt in her mind.

What type of worship and praise has God shown us that he enjoys? Perhaps physical limitations keep us from joining in Davidic dance worship, but has the Lord shown us other unique ways to "dance" before him? This week, let's take our dancing eyes and search for new ways to praise and worship him.

Elohey T'hilati, (God of my Praise), I want to dance before you with all my might (2 Sam. 6:14). If I'm able to actually dance, help me to overcome any obstacles that might keep me from joining in or from taking my worship to a new level.

If I'm unable to physically join in, show me how to "dance" in other ways. You are my Daddy, and I'm so grateful for your love and many blessings. Help me to take that thankfulness and channel it into new ways of praising and worshipping you! I love you! In Yeshua's Name. Amen

Let's take it to the Secret Place:

Have I ever danced before the Lord with all of my might? If so, please describe.

_____

_____

What does dancing mean to me?

_____

_____

_____

What could nonphysical dancing look like?

_____

_____

_____

_____

_____

End of Week Thirty-Seven:

Did I dance for the Lord? Did it deepen my relationship with him? If so, how?

_____

_____

_____

_____

Week Thirty-Eight ~ Loving Eyes

What Is God's Favorite Color?

"... I will be their God, and they will be my people. No longer will any of them teach his fellow community member or his brother, 'know ADONAI'; for all will know me, from the least of them to the greatest ..."

Jeremiah 31:31-34

I love my husband. After so many years of marriage, I think I know him pretty well, but he still surprises me nearly every day. We've weathered crises and challenges. Honestly, had we known what would happen we might have said, "See ya. Have a nice life!" and then run in opposite directions. Fortunately, God in his infinite mercy and wisdom doesn't give us a preview of the future.

Sometimes it feels like my hubby and I share the same brain. We finish each other sentences, understand the archaic, occasionally silly codes we use for life and circumstances, and recognize when the other is scared, angry, sad, or lovey-dovey. Other times, I can look at him and wonder, "Who in the world is this man?"

My husband's favorite movie is Lord of the Rings. Other than sex, his favorite activity is researching pretty much anything, so he'd rather read technical magazines and books than a good novel or inspirational book. (I still don't get that.) His favorite color is blue, and the best day in his life is still the day that we were married. He has five years of college math, calculus, and other courses with numbers that I could never do, but he hates to balance the checkbook, so I do it. His greatest desire is to have his own business; as a corporate man for nearly twenty-five years, he longs to be independent, explore his creativity, and set his own hours and pace.

When it comes to compassion and a servant's heart, my spouse is my mentor—I still have much to learn from him. Probably the best way to describe his self-sacrifice is that he always offers me the biggest piece or the last bite of everything—even chocolate. He knows how much that last bit of chocolate means to me.

How well do we know God?

This week's passage, after all of these years, still makes me weepy. It's a peek into God's heart and longing; it seems his greatest longing is that we would know him.

Of course, he wants us to accept Yeshua as our atonement, to obey him, and to worship him, but above that, I believe he wants us to know him because when we do, we'll do all of the other things—not perfectly, but willingly and even eagerly.

This passage also speaks of God's New Covenant, which Yeshua ratified hundreds of years later. The New Covenant that we abide under today is steeped in the longing of the Creator of the Universe.

This week's theme is simple, but it's our lifelong focus.

Let's ask the Lord to show us how we can know him better and help fulfill his longing. We do that not to add to our doctrine, eschatology, or theology, but to know him like we know our best friend, our child, and our husband.

Y'Didi, (My Beloved), I'm still amazed that you know me so well, even better than anyone, including and probably especially myself, knows me. I'm equally amazed that you long for me to know you. I'll never be able to understand the depths of who you are, but Lord, I want to begin to explore you in new ways—more like a lover and best friend. I'm not sure how this will work out practically, but I'm excited to begin this journey with you. I love you. In Yeshua's Name.

Let's take it to the Secret Place:

Who is the closest and best friend I have? Describe the relationship—
what I know about this person and what they know about me.

_____

_____

_____

_____

_____

_____

_____

Beginning with the attributes of this relationship, how can I apply them
to knowing the Lord better?

_____

_____

_____

_____

End of Week Thirty-Eight:

What new thing did I learn about the Lord in our Secret Place? Has
this changed my perception of him in any way? How?

_____

_____

_____

_____

Week Thirty-Nine ~ Fragrant Eyes

What's That Fragrance You're Wearing?

> "... [F]or to God we are the aroma of the Messiah ... [W]e are the sweet smell of life leading to more life."
>
> 2 Corinthians 2:15-16

An old slave woman stoked the last small fire. She bowed toward Hadassah and then backed out of the room. Hadassah chewed her lip and looked in the direction of the other young women in the room. They whispered among themselves. Hadassah was certain they shared the same question in her mind, "What is going to happen next?"

The girls modestly clutched the beautiful woven robes around their naked bodies and looked at the little stoves suspended over the burning coals. Another slave appeared with an armful of handsome-jeweled jars and poured different oils into each of the stoves. Soon, a delicious symphony of fragrances floated about the room—sandalwood, myrrh, cloves, and roses.

Hadassah took a few steps toward the burners. She closed her eyes and inhaled deeply. The loud clang of the door opening startled her. The other women squealed like frightened children. Hegai, the custodian of the king's women, boldly strode into the room followed by several older women.

He stood akimbo in the center of the room and pointed a thick ringed-finger toward Hadassah.

"You, Esther," he called her by her Persian name.

She bowed slightly. Hegai nodded toward a slave who quickly moved to a fire pit. He smiled at Hadassah and then spoke tenderly.

"Listen to old Omeed. She will instruct you."

Hegai lifted his chin toward the group of girls huddled together.

"Today, you all begin the twelve months of preparation."

The custodian of the king's women turned and left as abruptly as he had arrived.

Without ever raising her eyes toward Hadassah, Omeed explained that this particular stove contained oil of sandalwood.

She whispered, "The king's favorite."

The old woman explained how Hadassah should crouch over the stove and cover herself from the top of her head to her toes with her cloak. In this tent, the heat would open her pores, allowing the fragrance of the oil to be absorbed into her skin, hair, clothing, and pores. Only when the coals cooled could she move away.

Hadassah wondered how she could do this for the next twelve months. As she tried to find a comfortable position over the steaming stove and covered herself in the royal robes, she hoped that indeed as she absorbed his favorite fragrance, she would be pleasing to her king.

Do we absorb the fragrance of Yeshua until it becomes a part of us?

Karon watched the nurse insert the bolus of chemicals into the IV. Her practiced hands moved efficiently and carefully. Karon smiled and attempted to catch Nurse Kashani's eye, but, as usual, the nurse didn't make eye contact.

When the nurse finished, she briefly looked in Karon's direction. "I'll be back in a half-hour."

"Thank you, Nurse—"

Karon didn't finish her gratitude before Ms. Kashani made her hasty exit.

Karon shrugged. It wasn't that the woman was outright rude, but somehow Karon sensed the nurse was uneasy around her despite her efforts to be friendly. The other nurses were friendlier and sometimes stayed a few extra minutes with her during the therapy.

She said a quick prayer for the nurse and that the drugs entering her bloodstream would fight the disease inside her. With her free hand, she put in her ear buds and turned on her i-pod. She'd downloaded several of her praise and worship CDs onto it. Settling herself as comfortably as possible into the hospital's recliner, she closed her eyes and allowed the music and chemicals to do their jobs.

This was month three of Karon's chemotherapy. She was halfway through the constant bitter taste, nausea, vomiting, hair loss, and lethargy and on her way to overcoming her stage-three Hodgkin's disease. Karon still wondered how she, a health-conscious woman of thirty, could get cancer, but apparently, it wasn't all that uncommon.

A few minutes into the therapy, the queasiness crescendoed. Karon yanked out the ear buds, moved the large trashcan closer, and heaved. Her mind also pushed out a litany of thoughts, "How undignified. Oh, Lord have mercy! Have the doctors ever tried this stuff on themselves? I can do all things through the Messiah, who strengthens me. Why me, Lord? You are my Rock, Lord. Help me."

After finishing several rounds of sickness, she sat back exhausted. With a shaking hand, she worked the ear buds back in. "Thank you, Lord, that you are my strength and shield."

The last day of therapy finally arrived. Carrying a small bouquet of daisies that she'd picked from her garden, Karon walked into the chemo room and found Nurse Kashani tidying up the room. "Hmm, this isn't her usual shift," Karon thought. She had intended them as a gift for another nurse with whom she'd developed a friendship. Oh well.

"Nurse Kashani, after today you'll be rid of me." Karon smiled broadly and extended the bunch of flowers. "Here, these came from my garden. Thank you for taking such good care of me."

Dark brown eyes searched Karon's eyes like a starving child.

The intensity of the nurse's gaze made Karon's heart beat rapidly. She didn't quite know what to say, and the nurse didn't appear to be forthcoming with what was going on in her head.

Finally, releasing her intent look, Nurse Kashani took the daisies and left the room muttering a quiet, "Thank you."

Karon wasn't sure if she had offended the woman or what. "Who was going to hook her up to the chemo?" she thought. She sat in the recliner and waited. Someone cleared her throat. Karon looked up to see Nurse Kashani smiling at her. Smiling. Without a word, she performed her usual tasks except from time to time the nurse made eye contact with Karon.

Once she finished, Ms. Kashani pulled a chair toward Karon and then sat in it. She leaned forward and said, "May I stay with you?"

Karon felt warmth throughout her body. She knew God was giving her a precious gift. She opened her IV'd hand toward the woman.

"That would be wonderful, Nurse Kashani."

The nurse placed her hand in Karon's.

"Please call me Rashia."

"Please call me Karon."

Rashia's eyes moistened and then looked down.

"Karon, why do you sing?"

Yeshua warned that we would have trials—circumstances that heat things up in our lives and open our spiritual pores. What fragrance saturates those open pores—our Messiah's or the world's?

This week, as we reflect on the goodness of Yeshua and all that he has done for us, let's create a tent and steep ourselves in his fragrance. If we are currently in a trial, know that our pores are open. Let's pray that we immerse ourselves in him and become a pleasing aroma to the Lord and to those tired of this world's odor.

Oh my Comforter, my Shalom (Peace), I want to be a pleasing aroma to you, dear Lord. Am I? Are others drawn to Yeshua's scent in me? This week, show me any stinky areas of my life, and help me to soak in the fragrance of Yeshua.

During this trial I'm going through right now, I know I have a choice: to steep in your presence or the world's. Show me how this works. Please show me how to incorporate this into my life every day whether or not I am in tribulation. I so love you. In Yeshua's Name. Amen

Let's take it to the Secret Place:

Am I in a trial right now? Describe. If not, describe a past trial and its outcome.

_____

_____

_____

_____

_____

Was I a pleasing aroma to the Lord? Were others drawn to Yeshua's scent? Why?

_____

_____

_____

_____

List the ways that God is showing me how to create a tent and soak in his fragrance.

_____

_____

_____

_____

_____

_____

_____

End of Week Thirty-Nine:

Did I begin learning how to beautify myself for the King? How is this affecting my relationship with him?

_____

_____

_____

_____

Week Forty ~ Awe-filled Eyes

Still Seeing the Wonder

"Happy is the person who is never without fear [always in a state of awe], but he who hardens his heart will fall into misfortune."

Proverbs 28:14

Ida walked along the bike path as her granddaughter, Bina, rode her tricycle. After a half-hour, they had barely gone a few yards and the Bubbe (grandmother) was about ready to carry the tricycle and Bina to the playground.

"Oh, look, Bubbe!" Bina stopped again and pointed toward a tree. "See the birdie? What's he doing?"

After a deep cleansing breath, Ida stood next to the little girl.

"That's a woodpecker, Bina. Come on, let's get going. You want to have time to play on the swing before dinner, right?"

Her curly mop nodded, but she didn't move.

Rat-tat-tat-tat! The woodpecker drilled enthusiastically into the tree.

Her granddaughter's eyes widened.

"What's that?"

Ida smiled.

"That's the woodpecker. She's looking for food inside the tree."

Bina climbed off her bike and took Ida's hand.

"Does it hurt the birdie, Bubbe?"

The two never made it to the playground. They sat in the grass and watched the birds, squirrels, and tall trees swaying in the breeze. Ida marveled at Bina's observations and questions about the animals and plant life. The two made up silly songs about the woodpecker looking for macadamia nuts to give to the squirrels.

As they headed back to Ida's house, Bina was quiet as she pedaled beside Bubbe. Ida couldn't remember the last time she'd simply sat and had fun with her granddaughter instead of keeping her occupied with games and activities. When was the last time she'd taken time to enjoy the beautiful scenery around her?

The most precious aspect was seeing it all with the eyes of a child—the awe of God's miraculous creation. What joy, peace, and wonder were contained in those moments. What a gift.

"Bubbe?"

Ida looked at Bina's sweet, round face. She had stopped again.

"This was the best day of all. You're the smartest person in the whole wide world."

Bina took her grandmother's hand and kissed it; then, her little feet resumed their pedaling.

Bubbe wiped a tear, cleared the emotion from her throat, and said, "Thank you, Bina. It was my best day, too."

Are we still in awe of God? The dictionary defines awe as an overwhelming feeling of wonder or admiration.

This week, let's return to that childlike wonder that we had when we first accepted Yeshua. Remember that joy? That gratitude? Let's ask the Lord to show us how to restore the joy and awe of our salvation, of sitting in his presence, and of reflecting on Yeshua's commitment to our redemption. Ask him to bring back our eyes of awe.

Gili (My Delight), restore unto me the joy of your salvation (Ps. 51:12a), and restore my eyes of awe. Every day I will bless you; I will praise your name forever and ever! You are great and should be greatly praised (Ps. 145:2–3a)! Help me to return to you as in days of old. I love you! In Yeshua's Name. Amen.

Let's take it to the Secret Place:

When was the last time I sat in awe of God? Describe the circumstances, the setting, and the emotions I felt.

_____

_____

_____

_____

_____

_____

List the ways God is showing me how to recapture the awe of my relationship with him.

_____

_____

_____

_____

_____

End of Week Forty:

What happened in our Secret Place this week? Did I regain my eyes of awe? How has it affected our relationship?

_____

_____

_____

_____

Chapter Nine

Trusting Eyes

Trusting eyes see the obstacles before them—they acknowledge them—but depend on God to help work through those challenges in the Secret Place.

During the next five weeks, we'll search for eyes of commitment, reassurance, contentment, expectation, and faith. The Lord doesn't frown on our failures; he frowns when we give up. As we pursue this deeper sense of trusting, expect wonderful surprises from him along the way.

Week Forty-One ~ Commited Eyes

The Pursuit of Joy

> *"It is good for me that I have been afflicted, that I may learn your statutes."*
>
> Psalm 119:71 (NKJV)

The movie *The Pursuit of Happyness*[1] was based on the real-life story of Chris Gardner, who interned for a stock-brokerage firm while homeless and taking care of his young son. I have to admit watching it in the theater was a little like getting a root canal—a painful but necessary experience.

Trial after trial fell on this man as he tried to educate himself to build a more stable life for himself and his son. I kept thinking there's no way that he could handle another setback, disappointment, or rejection. Yet, another incident happened, and he did handle it.

Unlike the tenacious Chris Gardner, do we too easily give up when life, the enemy, or even a test from God drips, drowns, or devastates us? Do we have eyes of commitment even when it feels like God is not committed to us?

The emergency room clock mocked Hannah's family's concern. For the past hour, Hannah's lungs rode one wave of severe asthma attack after another. Now, the young woman's breathing had stopped altogether. The doctor paced nervously. Hannah's husband sat in silent panic. Hannah wondered how long a person could go without breathing. She wondered if this was it—if Yeshua was taking her now.

As Hannah waited, she felt a warmth and peace. She closed her eyes, ready to die.

No. It's not time. Pursue the things that I show you during this season of affliction.

Hannah gasped and cringed against the pain as her lungs filled with air. Her husband wrapped her in his arms until the doctor gently untangled the relieved man from his wife. Although Hannah still struggled to breathe, the emergency room doctor seemed pleased with her vital signs. Once stable, she was sent home with medications and a warning to see her family doctor for more tests.

Prior to that night, Hannah had never had asthma; now, she struggled with multiple attacks every week, and no one could figure out the triggers. She never knew when an episode would occur.

Hannah's life became very restrictive. Her doctors relegated the once active woman to a quiet life at home and at times to her bed. She had to depend on the kindness of her congregation to help her with house-cleaning, cooking, and taking care of her family. But Hannah remembered the words of the Lord: Pursue the things I show you during this season of affliction.

With all of the solitary time, Hannah committed to learning what God wanted to show her. She learned that she had a deep-rooted fear, which produced anxiety and stress. She learned that even when her body was weak, her prayers and intercessions were strong on behalf of family and friends. Hannah learned that her pursuit of the joy in the Lord was her strength. She grew passionate in her pursuits to know him better.

For years, Hannah has journeyed the road of poor health. Her hopeful message to others with chronic diseases or disorders (whether emotional or physical) is that this is the most precious time of her life. She has never felt more alive and connected with her Healer.

In the midst of hardships, do we have eyes committed to our Lord—even if he chooses not to heal us? Or are we discouraged and have doubts of God's commitment to us? This week, let's allow the Holy Spirit to examine our eyes and ask him to help us strengthen our commitment to him.

Adonai Rafa (Lord who Heals), you know I need healing for _____. You have heard my prayers and many others' prayers. I know you aren't ignoring me. I know you are as committed to me now as you are when you heal me—whenever you choose to do this. But in the meantime, Lord, I choose to increase my commitment to you.

I want to passionately pursue you, to know you better, to know me better, and to clean out any sins in my life that keep me from a closer relationship with you. I don't do this to earn my healing; I do this because I love you. In Yeshua's Name. Amen.

Let's take it to the Secret Place:

Have I ever or am I now going through a physical, emotional, or spiritual hardship? Describe.

_____

_____

_____

Have I ever felt ashamed of my affliction? Why?

_____

_____

_____

How has the Lord shown his commitment to me? How have I shown my commitment to him?

_____

_____

_____

_____

End of Week Forty-One:

Did the Lord and I work together to strengthen my eyes of commitment? How did this affect my relationship with him?

_____

_____

_____

_____

Week Forty-Two ~ Contented Eyes

Am I Too Needy?

> *"Surely I have calmed and quieted my soul, Like a weaned child with [her] mother; Like a weaned child is my soul within me."*
>
> *Psalm 131:2 (NKJV)*

*E*ver watch hungry babies waiting for their mother's breast or a bottle? They'll scrunch up their little eyes and cry like someone has pinched them. If their eyes are open, they get more frantic instead of calming down when they see the bottle or breast. On the other hand, a weaned child has learned that she will be fed. Her need doesn't outweigh her confidence in her mother's love. She is content to rest in her mother's arms without being fed.

Can we rest in the Lord's arms without always needing to be fed? Do we trust that he will care for us?

"Calm down, Shula." The teenager's mother fanned her fingers on the kitchen counter and leaned toward her daughter. "You'll make yourself sick with all of this worry."

Shula felt a flush of indignation heat her face.

"Whatever!"

She climbed off the stool, huffed to her room, and then slammed the door. Shula threw herself onto her canopy bed, which shot her teddy bear into the air and to the floor.

"Teddy!"

Shula reached down to rescue her old friend. She cuddled it tightly with streams of tears flowing down her cheek.

"At least you care. You wouldn't believe the day I've had. The week! The year!" Shula moaned loudly and buried her face in Teddy's fur. She shouted into his soft body. "I hate my life! Why are you punishing me, God?"

A soft knock interrupted Shula's tempestuous sanctuary. She wiped her nose on her sleeve.

"What?"

Her mother's muffled voice sounded far away, "May I come in?"

"It's open."

Shula rolled to her side to face the wall, not her mother's prying eyes. She felt the bed give as her mother sat on the edge.

Her mother sighed.

"Shula, honey, look at me."

Shula flopped to her back, then crossed her arms tightly over her chest, and stared at the pink and purple rosebuds of her canopy. Her mother sighed again.

"I didn't mean to hurt your feelings, Shula. I know you're concerned about making the cheerleading squad and honor roll again this year. This is your last year of high school, and I know you want to be accepted into Temple University."

Shula's wall of anger crumbled into sobs.

"Mom, it's terrible. Today, Andrea told me that there was no way I'd make the squad, and I have a big calculus test and have to prepare a speech for—"

Her mother placed a hand on Shula's forehead.

"Shula, honey, stop. Listen to yourself."

Shula shoved her mother's hand away.

"Fine. Just go away. You don't care about me."

The bed moved again. Her mother stood, and Shula felt the loss of her presence. "I knew she didn't really care," Shula thought.

"Shula, God has given you many gifts. Brains, athleticism, and the desire to be the best that you can be."

Shula felt a "but" coming.

"But he didn't give you fear, worry, or confusion." Her mother gently jiggled her shoulder. "Sit up."

The teenager sat up and wrapped her arms around her knees. Her mother sat back down on the bed.

"Honey, you're old enough now to trust that God is in control."

Shula rolled her eyes.

"I know he's in control, Mom. It's just that he doesn't talk to me and tell me what's going to happen. I need to know if I made the squad, if I will pass my test, or if I will get into college next year. Is that so wrong?"

Her mother patted her knees.

"Of course, we want to know the answers to all of our questions, but part of believing that God is in control is resting in him even when we don't have those answers. Scooch over, Shully."

Shula moved over and let her mom sit by her. Shula snuggled into the circle of her mother's arms.

"Go to him, Shula. Trust him."

She sniffed, "How?"

"Study his Word like you study for your calc test. Practice praising him like you practice cheers when you feel those confusing, scary feelings. Pray with understanding that he is in control of your destiny."

Shula closed her eyes. She guessed God, and her mom, did care.

Do we sometimes doubt God's sovereignty and love? Do we find ourselves going to him more often in frantic need of something? This week, let's work on contented eyes even in the midst of troubles, confusion, and unanswered questions.

El Shaddai (God Almighty), I'm sorry for being so needy over _____. Wean me from my neediness. This week, train me up to be content even in the midst of unsettling circumstances. In Yeshua's Name. Amen.

Let's take it to the Secret Place:

Am I needy? Sometimes? Most of the time? Why?

_____

_____

_____

_____

_____

_____

What happens to my body and emotions when this neediness comes over me? This week, try to record incidents where I felt like this.

_____

_____

_____

_____

_____

_____

Here is how I combated this neediness with contented eyes.

_____

_____

_____

_____

End of Week Forty-Two:

Am I better able to recognize when I don't trust the Lord? Was I able to practice using contented eyes even in challenging circumstances? How?

_____

_____

_____

_____

Week Forty-Three~ Expectant Eyes

Who Knew Turning Fifty and a Having a Hysterectomy Would Provide One of My Top Ten Best Vacations?

> *"My soul, wait silently for God alone, for my expectation is from him."*
>
> Psalm 62:5 (NKJV)

I don't like surprises. I'm a planner and list-maker. At one time, I was known to add a completed task to my list just so I could cross it off. Some call it compulsive; I call it record keeping.

Perhaps it's because I like being in control. I like life running smoothly on all eight cylinders. An occasional bump is doable but not too disruptive, or my busy schedule will collapse on top on me.

That's why six months before my fiftieth birthday when I realized that I needed a hysterectomy—Oy vey iz mir (Woe is to me)—I wondered how I could stop my busy world for six weeks of recovery. What kind of jubilee birthday present was this?

Questions tumbled in my brain like a monkey wrench in a clothes dryer. What would the surgery and going under anesthesia be like? What if they gave me too much or not enough? What in the world would the office do without me? What would I do without the office? How could I keep from going nuts while I was staying in bed for weeks? Oy! Didn't God know how much I disliked surprises? The unknown?

Once I took a breath, the Lord gave me a picture of what the convalescence time might be like if I trusted him. He promised it would be our time together, and he had surprises that he promised I would love.

Okay, I still did some planning. My husband would stay with me in the hospital, my mother intended to fly in after I returned home, the ladies from my congregation had delicious meals scheduled to be delivered right to our kitchen, and I made arrangements for several people to fill in for me at the office. The surgery and healing time didn't seem so daunting. In fact, I was beginning to look forward to it.

At my fiftieth birthday party, through the women who organized the party, the Lord showered his love for me. The event was complete with a skit, poem, and special song. The love and effort of these women humbled me, and I laughed until my sides hurt.

A few weeks later, I had the hysterectomy. The operation was not a breeze—abdominal surgery isn't fun—yet I truly felt God's presence. The recuperation time was amazing and restful. I mostly let go and enjoyed days and weeks of just being. It was so unlike me.

I thought I'd be bored, but God came through with the promise of little surprises—precious intimate moments that I still treasure today. The experience surpassed my expectations. His surprises were so much better than anything I could have planned.

Do I still like to plan and be in control? Yes. However, I'm not as bad as I was before. I try not to be so busy, so scheduled, and so planned that I overlook his surprises. I'm learning—albeit slowly—how to have more quiet moments to let my expectations for the day be him and what he has for me. I need to trust him for the big and small details and the planned and unplanned circumstances.

Does my story make your skin crawl? Are you so not a planner? Do you feel like you're always playing catch-up? Not sure what you should do first each day? Allowing the Lord to plan your days can be just as much of a challenge. Really, planners and non-planners can share the same issue, trust—trusting him with our days and our expectations.

This week, let's ask the Lord to show us where we so tightly hold on to our plans and schedules or become distracted with too many choices that we miss his surprises. Let's work on trusting him for our expectations.

Adonai Haiyai (God of my Life), this week, please help me to exercise my trusting muscle. I want to experience more of your surprises. Help me rest and abide more deeply in you so that my expectations come from you. In Yeshua's Name. Amen.

Let's take it to the Secret Place:

Am I a planner or anything-goes person? How do I handle a typical day?

_____

_____

_____

_____

_____

Describe a time or day when the Lord surprised me with a wonderful incident. What did I do differently at the time?

_____

_____

_____

_____

_____

Describe an event this week. Did I purposely leave myself open for God's surprise?

_____

_____

_____

_____

End of Week Forty-Three:

Was I able to trust the Lord enough to surprise me? Was I able to practice using expectant eyes even during a busy day? How?

_____

_____

_____

_____

Destiny Interrupted

> *"But [Moses] replied, 'Please, LORD, send someone else——anyone you want!'"*
>
> *Exodus 4:13*

Where was the proud Prince of Egypt, the man of destiny who thought he could save his Jewish brethren by killing one Egyptian? Over there—watching his father-in-law's sheep.

As a younger man, Moses felt assured in his destiny as the deliverer of his people (Acts 7:25), but he failed miserably in his own attempts to fulfill that destiny. Fleeing to the desert, he'd been humbled to a career considered an abomination (Gen. 46:34), to the royalty that had raised him.

At last, Moses made his peace with his life and his new family. The cries of his people were far from him and so were the memories of his failure.

Then, a burning bush caught his eye, and all of the old memories caught up with Moses. God was calling Moses back to his destiny as his People's deliverer, and Moses was scared. The Lord intended to imbue Moses with his power to perform great wonders. But even the wonders were scary.

Maybe if God had turned Moses' rod into a long-stemmed rose or had had Moses pull a cute, fuzzy bunny from his cloak, Moses might not have tried to talk God out of enlisting him. The Lord tried to reassure Moses that he could serve as deliverer, but Moses didn't quite trust the Lord enough to overcome his fears.

Is our fear of failure so strong that we're afraid to step into the destiny to which God has called us?

Simone's first day back at work was a relief, but she never admitted that fact out loud. She was too ashamed. Although she couldn't reclaim her nice office, it was good to be in an environment that she understood and felt she could handle.

Here she wasn't a failure. Here what was required of her posed no challenge.

From the time she had been a little girl playing with dollies, she wanted children. After many years of trying, she finally got pregnant. A few weeks before Lian was born, she tendered her resignation, ready for fulltime motherhood.

Who knew she'd be a lousy mother?

Her husband had tried to encourage her, but what did he know? He was a confident man on the road as much as he was home. He wasn't around to see half of her failures and insecurities as a mom.

He hadn't even questioned her when she had announced her decision to return to the workplace. His easy acceptance seemed to confirm that he felt she was inept at a woman's most natural role.

Apparently, God had neglected to give her the maternal gene.

Back in her comfortable environment as she lost herself in spreadsheets and calculations, she relaxed. Numbers made sense; they were predictable.

When Simone happened to glance at the expensively framed studio photo of her daughter on her desk, she pushed back the guilt of abandoning her to a stranger. But the nanny seemed to have a better understanding of her daughter's needs. "Best to leave those things to professionals," she reasoned. "Isn't that why my clients seek me for their accounting needs?"

Still, the conflict churned inside her. What kind of woman was she? Simone had failed miserably at nursing and was devastated when the doctor suggested she should put the baby on a bottle. Simone felt so rejected when her daughter seemed to prefer it to her breast. The woman who seldom failed at anything in her career couldn't distinguish between Lian's cries of hunger, pain, and sleepiness. She constantly changed a dry diaper or forced a bottle between her daughter's little pink lips. "What kind of mother falls asleep while feeding her baby at night? What if I had rolled over and suffocated her?"

When Simone returned home later that first day back at work, Lian was bathed, fed, and ready for bed. The nanny handed Lian to Simone and in a detached manner began reading a summary of Lian's day, which had included the child's developmental progress.

As the nanny closed her journal, she looked at Simone, "Oh, yes, and Lian giggled today."

"I missed Lian's first laugh," she thought. Simone looked down at the angelic face of her daughter. Lian yawned and smiled contentedly at her mother. Simone's heart lurched. "What am I doing?"

That night, Simone tossed and turned. Finally, she woke up her husband and told him about all of her insecurities and shame.

He gathered Simone in his arms, "I wondered why you went back to work, Simone. For as long as I've known you, you've always wanted children. We've been planning this for years."

Simone nodded, not trusting her voice to speak.

"Do you want to resign from your job?"

Simone's stomach knotted.

"I don't think I'm ready for fulltime motherhood."

Her husband squeezed her shoulders.

"Let's pray."

Simone decided to work part-time. She opened up to several women in her congregation and received emotional and spiritual support as she learned how to be a good mommy to Lian.

When Simone became pregnant with her second child, she quit her job and embraced her destiny as mother to Lian and Joshua.

Moses' insecurities and fears were not a match for God's grace. God worked with Moses to overcome the fears. Eventually, Moses fully embraced his destiny and accepted God's reassurances that he would provide all Moses needed to do the seemingly insurmountable tasks before him.

Do we know our destiny? Have we shelved our calling because we tried to fulfill the calling on our own and failed miserably? Are we ready to explore with the Lord what our call truly involves and trust him to teach and prepare us?

Whether our callings are for ministry, advanced schooling for a professional career, painting, sculpting, writing, speaking, or teaching, this week, let's allow him to reassure us of that calling and show us the steps that we need to take to walk in our destiny. Let's trust the Lord to bring us back from our interruption of his destiny in his perfect timing.

Adonai Yireh (Lord Provider), I believe you have called me to _____.

Please forgive me for any attempts to fulfill this calling on my own. Please forgive me for wanting to give up. I'm ready to listen and prepare for the time when you will release me to this destiny. I know I'm ill equipped on my own, but you will supply all that I need. In Yeshua's Name. Amen.

Let's take it to the Secret Place:

Do I know my calling/destiny? If yes, describe.

_____

_____

_____

_____

_____

Am I living the life to which I think God called me? How?

_____

_____

_____

_____

_____

Is there anything I was once passionate about that I've shelved over the years? If so, what?

_____

_____

_____

_____

End of Week Forty-Four:

Did the Lord communicate to me about my calling? Did it draw me closer to him? How?

_____

_____

_____

_____

Week Forty-Five ~Faithful Eyes

Pushing Through

> ""With you I can run through a whole troop of men, with my God I can leap a wall!"
>
> Psalm 18:29

I struggle with giving up. You know, in the fatalistic sense: "What's the use?"

It's not that I'm not a hard or dedicated worker, but there seems to be an invisible wall that sometimes pops out to block me achieving a greater level of commitment or victory. This manifests itself in relationships, my job, and goals that I've set for myself.

For many years, I couldn't identify this wall—I didn't know it existed—until I had our daughter.

Labor and delivery isn't for the faint of heart. It's the greatest example I know of pushing (literally and figuratively) through. Because I'm not a stoic, I did as much research as I could about childbirth. (By the way, ladies, there were no epidurals then. Not only were they not available, but also the military hospital that I was going to didn't believe in pampering mothers. You grinned, bore it, and better not complain.) My husband and I practiced the Lamaze method until he could do it in his sleep. I'd convinced myself I was fully prepared by the time my water broke on June 19th.

I did pretty well during labor in spite of the fact that my hubby wasn't there. He was still on his ship—which was still at sea. When it came time to push, however, I pushed like I had practiced in Lamaze. But guess what? This was not practice; this was the real thing, and my delicate push wasn't nearly enough to bring my daughter into this world. I panicked. "This job is too big for me," I thought.

Then, I locked eyes with the nurse who called out, "Push hard, Terri. Now!"

I let go and pushed with everything in me. It was the first time that I had fully engaged emotionally and physically into an undertaking. The part of me that always held something back didn't. I had no choice.

And our beautiful daughter was born. What a wonderful reward. It was years before I put this experience into perspective in my spiritual life.

How many times had I quit because I believed something was just too difficult? How many times had I convinced myself that something was not God's will because of the challenges? How many times did I hold a part of me in reserve and wasn't willing to completely surrender to God? Was my struggle with the challenge or trusting the Lord?

Do you share my struggle? Is there a wall that stops you from overcoming, abiding in a deeper relationship, or completing a task? This week, let's ask the Lord for faithful eyes that can identify where we stop short and that he will help us see that there is no better choice than to completely trust him who is faithful in all circumstances.

El Ne-eman (Faithful God), how many times have I just given up rather than searching you out with faithful eyes? I'm tired of giving up in defeat. Help me to obliterate from my thoughts the phrase, "What's the use?" Instead, help me to leap over or push through the walls that keep me from experiencing a deeper relationship with you or others. Please help me to quit quitting and learn to follow through and complete the tasks to which you've called me or I've committed. I want to have faithful eyes toward you and be faithful in what I do by your strength and will. In Yeshua's Name. Amen.

Let's take it to the Secret Place:

Are there walls that keep me from moving forward? If so, please describe them.

_____

_____

_____

_____

_____

_____

Journal any incidents where I gave up rather than pushed through. Describe how I felt after my decision to quit.

_____

_____

_____

_____

_____

_____

Journal any incidents where I pushed through. Describe how that felt.

_____

_____

_____

_____

_____

End of Week Forty-Five:

Did I exercise faithful eyes this week? How has that affected my relationship with the Lord?

_____

_____

_____

_____

Chapter Ten

Passionate Eyes

Our lives are a balancing act. We have a choice to gravely and meticulously walk the line or pirouette, cartwheel, and dance the same narrow path.

In the Secret Place of safety, God wants us to discover who he created us to be. Even if we stumble, he's there to dust us off and encourage us to try again. He longs for us to be passionate about him and the lives and gifts he's given us.

During the next seven weeks, we'll learn how passionate our Beloved is for us and how he longs for us to be passionate about him. Our eyes will reveal the surprises of our hearts; we'll look for the vision God has for us; we'll soar with a God who likes to fly; we'll learn a new definition of being balanced; we'll discover how to have purely passionate eyes and begin applying these passions in our day-to-day lives.

God has created us as passionate beings. He longs for us to share in his passions. Are we ready?

Week Forty-Six ~ Revealing Eyes

Color Me Surprised

" . . . No eye has seen, no ear has heard, and no one's heart has imagined all the things God has prepared for those who love him."

1 Corinthians 2:9

God wants to surprise us. He likes blessing us with little gifts that make us smile and big gifts that make us shout for joy.

Picture how the Lover of our Soul longs to fulfill our heart's longings. Now, relate this to our passage. There's a little twist here. The Scripture seems to imply that we don't fully comprehend what our longings are. Is it possible that we might miss out on these gifts because we only look for what we can imagine?

Shayna presented her husband with a list of her top ten Hanukkah gifts. It wasn't that she was greedy—nothing extravagant was on the list—they were just practical things that she needed. History had proven that her husband apparently didn't have a clue. Shayna didn't want a repeat of last year's fiasco where she had had to give an Academy Award-worthy performance over a box of cutlery that she hadn't needed.

The first night of Hanukkah was frenzied. Shayna got home late from work. She dashed upstairs for a quick shower, rolled her hair, then ran to the kitchen in her robe, and pulled the brisket from the slow cooker. The usual peaceful candle-lighting[1] and dinner was a rushed affair. They were behind schedule to make it to services on time.

Shayna was anxious to finish dressing when her husband insisted that they exchange their gifts before they drove to synagogue. She pasted on a smile before pulling her gift for him from the buffet. Her husband opened his present and thanked her with a hug and kiss for the watch she had known that he needed.

With a wiggle of his eyebrows and Cheshire-cat grin, her husband reached into his pocket and pulled out a little velvet box. Shayna's heart dropped. "Oh no, he didn't get her another pair of earrings," she thought.

Despite the cliché that all women want jewelry, Shayna was much too sensible. She had two favorite pairs of earrings (everyday and dress). The rest gathered dust in her drawer until she could re-gift them to someone else. As she reached for the velvet box, a list of people to whom she could pass on the gift was already rolling through her head. Shayna prepared herself for another Oscar-worthy performance. The tightly hinged black box opened with a squeak.

Before her was the most beautiful diamond ring she had ever seen. It was the engagement ring that matched her wedding band—the ring that they'd never been able to afford.

Shayna screamed; not a nicely rehearsed exclamation but a spontaneous shout. Then, the tears fell like a waterfall.

Shayna looked at her husband in awe. She jumped from the table and threw herself into her husband's waiting arms. In spite of her unromantic appearance, they kissed passionately.

Although Shayna hadn't considered herself a jewelry person, this unexpected gift of love surprised and touched her in ways she never could have imagined.

Do we color our world with our own perceptions and miss the surprises that God has waiting for us? Do we think we know better—better than the Lover of our Soul—what will truly delight us? In our misconceptions about our true heart's needs, have we ever given away blessings that God meant for us?

Are we ready for something new and different from the Lord? Unexpected but glorious? This week, let's ask the Lord to teach us how to have eyes that reveal our hearts—the true hearts that God sees in us and to be open and vulnerable to any surprises he might want to give us.

Gili (My Delight), what do you have in store for me? I want to experience whatever it is you want me to experience. I don't want to pass up and turn away any surprise that you might have for me—whether extravagant or simple.

Frankly, I'm a little nervous and don't know what to expect. But I do trust you. I know you love me. I can't even imagine what little treasures— unexpected blessings that show me you know my heart—you have in store for me. I have a feeling, Lord, that as my eyes see more clearly into my heart, others will see you more clearly. What a blessing that would be! I love you, Lord. In Yeshua's Name. Amen.

Let's take it to the Secret Place:

Did God ever really surprise me? If so, please describe.

_____

_____

_____

_____

_____

_____

Were there times when I missed out on God's surprises? Or times when he tried to bless me, but I gave it away? Describe how that felt.

_____

_____

_____

_____

This week, journal any unexpected surprises and blessings that God gives me. Describe what I felt.

_____

_____

_____

_____

_____

End of Week Forty-Six:

This week, did my eyes reveal any of my true heart? How did that affect my relationship with the Lord?

_____

_____

_____

_____

True to the Vision

"Then ADONAI answered me; he said, write down the vision clearly on tablets, so that even a runner can read it. For the vision is meant for its appointed time . . ."

Habakkuk 2:2-3a

Goldie buttoned her gray cardigan sweater and smoothed the pleats of her wool skirt. She gathered her purse and Bible from the table next to the door. How Goldie looked forward to her Bible study with the ladies of the congregation. The rabbi's wife had such wonderful insights into Scripture, and the lively discussions inspired her.

As she started the car, she noticed that she was almost out of gas. Goldie looked at her watch. Now, she was going to be late.

Rather than stopping at her usual gas station, she chose one on the way to the synagogue. Goldie pulled up to full service section and dug through her purse to find her credit card.

A pimply face peered through her window.

"What can I do for ya, ma'am?"

"Fill it, please."

The young man made a ruckus as he inserted the nozzle. He whistled as he began washing her windows. Goldie sighed and stared at her watch again.

"Hey, you believe in that stuff?" Goldie startled. "What?" He pointed to her Bible lying on the passenger seat. "That Bible stuff. You believe all that?" She bristled. "Of all the impertinence," she thought. "Of course, I believe it—every single word." He shrugged a bony shoulder. "I was just asking, that's all. He returned to his whistling and washing.

Goldie tapped her foot and glanced at her watch. She wondered whether he would move any slower blindfolded and shackled.

Finally, she paid, turned up her praise and worship CD, put the car in gear, and pulled back onto her route. "Good," she thought. "I'll only be a few minutes late."

Go back.

Goldie's stomach felt like a flock of butterflies had been disturbed. Waves of conviction rolled in.

Go back and talk to that young man.

She pulled into a shopping center parking lot and put the car into park. Hardly daring to breathe, she laid her forehead on the steering wheel.

"Lord?" Goldie grasped the wheel tightly. "I thought those days were gone. I'm not a kid anymore. I don't have the stamina or the courage or—"

Go back.

She remembered the days of sharing the Good News downtown and of Jewish people screaming and spitting at her, grabbing her fliers, and throwing them away. Back then she was too naive to realize how dangerous it was to serve as a radical witness in that neighborhood. Back then, Goldie couldn't get enough of it.

She raised her head.

"But I'm going to miss Bible study, Lord. You want me to study your—"

The weak excuse died on her tongue. She put the car in reverse and backed out. Goldie prayed as she made her way back to the gas station. She parked her car at the side of the building and got out. The pimply-faced man looked her way.

"Pardon me, young man. May I do a better job of answering your question?"

Has time dulled our visionary eyes? Or has someone discouraged us in pursuing the vision that God has called us to?

This week, let's ask the Lord to clear our eyes of anything that might keep us from seeing his vision for our lives. Whether it's sharing the Good News, teaching Shabbat school, intercession, counseling, lecturing, studying, or whatever unique inspiration that he's given us, let's ask him to renew and refresh it. Then, take it to a deeper level.

El Zokher (God who Remembers), I know you have a vision for me on this Earth. Before I was even born, you knew what that vision was. In fact, you fashioned me to fulfill it by your will and guidance. Lord, time, circumstances, trials, and tribulations can cloud the visionary eyes that you gave me. Please help me to clean them of anything that distorts or blinds me. Show me where I've missed opportunities so that I can repent. Help me forgive anyone who might have unknowingly or knowingly discouraged me.

Also, Lord, I want to do these things in decency and order. Please raise up mentors to help me as I take these miraculous things to a new level. In Yeshua's Name. Amen

Let's take it to the Secret Place:

Do I know God's vision for me? If so, please describe.

_____

_____

_____

_____

Was there a time when I operated in the vision? Describe how that felt.

_____

_____

_____

_____

This week, write the vision that God has shown me for my life.

_____

_____

_____

_____

End of Week Forty-Seven:

This week, did God reveal or renew his vision for me? How has that affected my relationship with the Lord?

_____

_____

_____

_____

Week Forty-Eight ~ Pleasured Eyes

A Sweet Ride

The topic was obedience. Despite having the message handed to her on a spiritual plate by God himself, Joella still struggled with standing before a room full of women and delivering the lecture.

As the rabbi's wife introduced her, Joella's own battle with obedience was still fresh in her mind (see week fourteen), and she still yearned to give in to the impulse to run.

Joella remembered her last public introduction. She had stood on a swimmer's racing block as the announcer said her name and lane number. She didn't wave or acknowledge the audience around her—she was in game mode. Instead, she swung her arms like a windmill, shook her legs, and took giant gulps of air to prepare her lungs.

As the rabbi's wife spoke now, Joella looked at her shaking hands and smiled. Somehow, she didn't think swinging her arms like a windmill would work here.

The introduction was over, and a polite round of applause followed. Joella nodded and walked up to the podium with her pounding heart a 7.8 earthquake on the Richter scale. Alone on the platform, Joella looked out at the faces of the women she knew and loved. An awareness of God's great love for each woman sitting there—and for her—poured over her like warm chocolate fudge. The fog of fear lifted and in its place was clarity and joy.

Joella ran her hands along the sides of the wooden lectern. Her palms found their place and then grasped the edges. A surge went through her as though she held the steering wheel of a beautifully engineered sports car.

Gone were the anxiety, nervousness, fear, and incessant what-if scenarios. In their place was pleasure—complete ease and heart-racing pleasure at being at the wheel of this beautiful machine in his presence.

As she took the curves of each lesson and eased into the smooth ride of God's theme, she marveled at how right it felt. Joella also marveled that she didn't want the moment or experience to end.

Joella rounded the last corner of her message and finished by saying, "What the Lord has called you to do he will enable you to do. His ways are not heavy or burdensome. His yoke is easy. The rulings of the Lord are true and righteous, sweeter than honey. In obeying them, there is great reward."

Later, when Joella had a chance to reflect on the amazing experience, she realized that she had pleasured God by being obedient. But the most incredible surprise was how much he had pleasured her. God had placed her in the driver's seat of his destiny for her—and what a sweet ride it was.

Have we missed out on pleasured eyes because we are too afraid, too busy, or too uncomfortable to obey God's will and calling? Is it uncomfortable to think of our Bridegroom as the one who gives us pleasure? That he knows our secret longings and knows how to fulfill them?

This week, let's ask the Lord to show us how to pleasure him more with the understanding that he desires to pleasure us. Let's ask him to show us how to grab the steering wheel of his destiny for us—for the ride of our lives.

El Ahavah (God of Love), I want to pleasure you more deeply. Show me how. I want to be pleasured by you. Show me how to let go of anything that might keep me from knowing you in this intimate new way.

I've been learning more about the destiny that you have crafted for me. This is another level of discovery.

There are rooms in the bridal chamber that I have yet to explore. Take me there. I love you so. In Yeshua's Name. Amen.

Let's take it to the Secret Place:

Have I ever experienced the sweet ride of God? If so, please describe.

_____

_____

_____

_____

Have I ever turned away this ride? Describe how that felt.

_____

_____

_____

Journal moments of the drive with God and what it felt like to be pleasured by him.

_____

_____

_____

_____

End of Week Forty-Eight:

This week, did God pleasure me? Did I pleasure him? How has that affected our relationship?

_____

_____

_____

Week Forty-Nine ~Soaring Eyes

Flying With God

> "[And the LORD] rode upon a cherub, and flew; he flew upon the wings of the wind."
>
> Psalm 18:10 (NKJV)

A friend of mine once described his favorite recurring dream—it was about flying—not in a plane but like a bird. He sometimes tried to stay asleep so he could make himself dream of flying. He loved to feel the wind carry him up through the clouds and soar freely as the air sustained the weight of his body.

I know exactly what my friend expressed—the feeling of flying. Only it doesn't happen in my dreams, it happens sometimes when I write. Finding the marvelous place where a character's words for a novel or the message for an encouraging devotion seem to come from the heart of God. It's like soaring on an air current of God's inspiration and gliding effortlessly as I survey his beautiful scenery.

Believe it or not, I can have that same feeling when I analyze numbers and statistics. The seemingly dry, boring columns of numbers can reveal vital information that tells a hopeful or cautionary story that will benefit others. Many times, I've relished following a trail of information, like a bird flying home after winter's cold gives way to spring.

What makes you fly? Perhaps you don't think you should fly. What's the point?

God loves to soar. I believe he desires to take our hands so we can fly with him. He created us for flight. He created us for passion. What are you passionate about?

Breena loves the feel of dirt between her fingers and its deep musky scent. She loves the perfume of flowers and running her fingers over vividly colored petals. Each day, she gathers bouquets for her home. Many times, God reveals that friends and family also need a bit of color and beauty, so she delivers flowers to homes and hospitals.

Her vegetable garden brings a different level of pleasure as Breena tends to the vegetables' growth. Her harvest of veggies blesses her family, her neighbors, and the members of her congregation.

She calls the little plot behind her house "God's Garden of Lessons." It's also her Secret Place with him.

As she pulls the weeds that could choke and weaken her plants, she ponders how sin can choke and weaken her relationship with the Lord. When she prunes her rose bushes, she reflects on God's necessity for cutting away things in her life so that healthier and more fragrant flowers come forth. She understands seasons of growth and rest.

Nearly every day, Breena hears a little more of God's heart through his creation. In the solitude of working, she draws closer to him. Although she may sweat in the heat, swat at stinging insects, and lug heavy hoses to water in dry seasons, it's her passion. She soars with her Creator because they share the same passion.

What passions do you and the Lord share?

While caring for our families, sharing the Good News, and helping others are all worthwhile and pleasing to the Lord, this isn't the passion of which I'm speaking. It's the flying place that connects us with God—alone. It's our Secret Place. It's our place of passion where we can be the person he created us to be.

Whether that passion is carpentry, gardening, music, art, acting, medicine, gymnastics, cooking, video editing, singing, dancing, organizing, or any other unique attribute he has placed in us, find it.

This week, let's ask the Lord to show us how to fly with him. If you don't already know, ask him to show you the passions that he shares with you and that he longs to join with you in the Secret Place. If you do know your passions, take this week to more deeply connect with him; fly away with him—just the two of you.

For those seeking their passions:

     Abba, this concept is very new to me. I'm not exactly sure what my passions are, but I think it might be _____, _____, *or maybe both. It's a little scary to think of flying with you. But it's also thrilling. Will I know what it is when it happens? This week, I'm praying that you will reveal insights and clues to what this may be. I'm ready. In Yeshua's Name. Amen.*

For those who know their passions:

     Abba, revive and renew my passions, even those I haven't thought of in years. Anything that connects me more deeply with you is what I want to use. Thank you for creating parts in me that can unite me so profoundly with you. Let's go flying. I love you. In Yeshua's Name. Amen.

Let's take it to the Secret Place:

Have I ever flown with God? If so, describe that moment.

_____

_____

_____

_____

_____

Do I know what my passions are? Do I think I might know?
If so, describe them.

_____

_____

_____

_____

_____

Journal moments of flying with God.

_____

_____

_____

_____

_____

End of Week Forty-Nine:

This week, did God reveal or renew any passions? How has that affected our relationship??

_____

_____

_____

_____

How to Walk the Narrow Path

"... So Kefa [Peter] got out of the boat and walked on the water toward Yeshua. But when he saw the wind, he became afraid; and as he began to sink, he yelled, 'Lord! Save me!' Yeshua immediately stretched out his hand, took hold of him, and said to him, 'Such little trust! Why did you doubt?'"

Matthew 14:29–31

The gymnast gracefully mounted the balance beam with a flip off the springboard. Her choreographed routine included a series of full-twisting flip-flops, triple-turns, a forward- and back-flip, and finally an Arabian double-front dismount. Her landing was true and secure. The gymnast raised her arms in victory; the auditorium roared with applause.

After the crowd, officials, and other gymnasts had left the auditorium, the gymnast returned to the beam. Although she had competed well on the floor and uneven bars, her heart and mind favored the four-inch-wide piece of wood. She rubbed calloused hands over the smooth surface. When she was five, her first instructor called it the "narrow way." It wasn't until after the gymnast had accepted Yeshua as her Messiah that she understood what her teacher meant.

Back then, many in her congregation had felt the gymnast should quit her athletic pursuits. Some had believed it was prideful, and the costumes were too revealing. The gymnast prayed hard about that. She had called her first instructor for advice.

The instructor prayed with the gymnast and reminded her of the "narrow way."

"Remember the first time that you walked the beam?" her instructor asked. "I walked beside you as you learned to balance yourself walking on the constrictive piece of wood. I stood by you as you learned to stand on one foot and try more difficult moves."

The gymnast remembered the sense of security, the delight of learning something new, and the safety of learning in the presence of a skilled master who spotted her.

"That's how our walk is with the Lord. Truly we walk a narrow path, but God is with us—spotting us. Unfortunately, too many believe that the narrow way means we must live narrowly and constrictively."

Her instructor reminded her of the missionary Eric Liddle whose story was told in the movie Chariots of Fire.[2] More than a few dissenters felt his running distracted him from his spiritual calling. Eric's response, "I believe that God made me for a purpose ... [the mission], but he also made me fast, and when I run, I feel his pleasure."

"Feel his pleasure, my dear."

The gymnast felt God's pleasure. The career she chose was fraught with trials, temptations, and pain to her body. Still, she couldn't imagine living a narrow life without the joy and freedom God gave her—on and off of the beam.

Are we afraid of taking chances in our passions? Are we content with an effortless, undemanding, and painless path? This week's passage highlights Peter's attempt to walk on water. It's easy to take a scholarly approach and analyze Peter's lack of faith, but let's be honest, how many of us would have even tried?

Peter's time with Yeshua was full of hits and misses—many misses—but Yeshua was there to spot him. Notwithstanding all of the mistakes, including Peter's betrayal of Yeshua, Yeshua eventually imparted a great anointing on Peter. In the future, the apostle braved much more frightening experiences than a storm and gave great honor to the Lord.

Let's ask the Lord to reveal anything keeping us from having balanced eyes. Ask him to help us with any unbalanced attitudes and fears when it concerns our faith and our God-given passions.

Elohim K'rovim (Close God), is my spiritual walk and relationship with you too restrictive? Do I tend to take the easier options? Am I afraid to take chances in my pursuits of my passions with you?

If this is the case, I repent. Help me to press forward past the simple walking on the narrow beam and begin learning new graceful—and maybe even adventurous—movements. I know you're close by, spotting me. And even if I lose my balance or slip, you'll be right there to help me climb back up. I love you! In Yeshua's Name. Amen.

Let's take it to the Secret Place:

How am I like the gymnast? How am I like her critics?

_____

_____

_____

_____

_____

_____

Do I constrict my faith or God-given passions? If so, how does this manifest itself?

_____

_____

_____

_____

_____

Have I ever sensed God spotting me as I learn difficult moves?

_____

_____

_____

_____

_____

End of Week Fifty:

Did the Lord show me how to overcome any fears or unbalance attitudes? How has that affected our relationship ?

_____

_____

_____

_____

Week Fifty-One ~ Pure Eyes

Spiritual Lust

> "But if you have bitter envy and self-seeking in your hearts, do not boast and lie against the truth. This wisdom does not descend from above, but is earthly, sensual, demonic."
>
> James 3:14–15 (NKJV)

*D*iscovering our God-given passions is stimulating. For many of us, this has been a new concept. New vistas lay before us waiting to be explored. It can all be a little intimidating and overwhelming. We may feel a new sense of freedom with which we don't know what to do.

This week's message is critical as we enter these new territories.

The opposite of passion is lust. Passion seeks the person and a relationship; lust seeks what the person and relationship can give. We must be careful to maintain pure eyes and be especially vigilant for spiritual lust.

Helen wanted to run from the room. Clearly, these people didn't understand. "All I want to do is help. God has gifted me in this area. How can they not see that?" she thought. The director of Shabbat school sat across from Helen. The huge stack of papers representing months of Helen's efforts sat on a chair beside her.

"Helen, it's not that we don't want you to help with our program, but restructuring the entire curriculum is a pretty big task."

"She's just worried I'm trying to take over her job," Helen thought. Helen folded her arms across her chest.

"I've read through most of your proposal," the director continued placing her hand on the two hundred pages, "but what you're suggesting is too complex and expensive for our congregation." She reached over to pat Helen's hand. "Why not try teaching one of the classes or observe the different age groups for a while, and then you'll know better how to build a set of courses for our congregation."

Helen didn't make eye contact with the director. "I'll pray about it," she replied.

When they stood, Helen only limply hugged the director before leaving.

Helen *knew* she was supposed to write a new Shabbat school curriculum. "Why is leadership fighting me? Don't they know God wants me to do this? It is my passion to write for children," she reasoned. "I did hear from you, Lord, didn't I?" Helen's emotions vacillated between indignation and devastation. She had felt sure that God wanted her to write children's curriculum. Had she heard wrong?

Helen humbled herself in the Secret Place. Finally, she realized she had taken matters into her own hands instead of truly seeking God's release or timing, like a child who only partially listens to instructions. She acknowledged what she had done to the Lord.

Eventually, Helen took the director's advice and taught one of the Shabbat school classes. She gained a valuable practical understanding of what the department needed in the way of curriculum. In the meantime, she also took writing courses.

After several years, Helen presented a proposal for one of the grade levels. The teachers tested the program and helped Helen fine tune the curriculum. The children and teachers loved the new series and spread the word to other congregations.

Perhaps someday Helen will write for all age-levels, but until then, she hones her gift and attitude in the Secret Place.

Do we seek what God can do for us or through us rather than seek him? When others don't accept our talents or ideas, do we become offended? If our eyes become clouded by offense, perhaps we aren't God-seeking, but self-seeking. Are we in spiritual lust—where we crave what God can do for us rather than crave God?

This week, let's ask the Holy Spirit to examine our eyes for anything that clouds the pure eyes that God longs for us to have, especially as we explore our God-given passions.

Adonai Tsidkenu (the Lord our Righteousness), I take this warning seriously. I want my eyes to be pure and not clouded by my own self-seeking spiritual lusts. Dear Holy Spirit, reveal anything that corrupts the holy passions given to me. I'm excited about my deeper relationship with you. Help me to keep it in your holy perspective. In Yeshua's Name. Amen.

Let's take it to the Secret Place:

Have I ever given in to spiritual lust? How did that manifest itself?

_____

_____

_____

_____

Do I have a plan to keep my eyes pure? Describe.

_____

_____

_____

Journal my efforts to keep my eyes pure.

_____

_____

_____

End of Week Fifty-One:

Did the Lord show me how to keep my eyes pure? Did this deepen our relationship? If so, how?

_____

_____

_____

Week Fifty-Two ~ Practically Passionate Eyes

Living Our Passions

I am my beloved's, and my beloved is mine.

Song of Solomon 6:3a (NKJV)

A woman I deeply respect gave me a book, *I'm Not Suffering From Insanity ... I'm Enjoying Every Minute of It!*[3] (Given the fact that this lady knows all of my deep dark secrets, I've always wondered if she was trying to tell me something.) There's a chapter called "Practice Your Passions," which encourages believers to integrate their passions into their day-to-day lives. The author writes:

> What if we stopped listing our priorities and started living our passions? What would our lives be like then?
>
> Now don't get me wrong. I'm not saying we should neglect our responsibilities. I'm not advocating that we abandon our obligations. And I'm certainly not suggesting that we live for ourselves and pursue only what feels good in light of our whims and desires.
>
> Not at all. Instead, I'm suggesting that we pinpoint our passions and we use them to accomplish our goals, dreams and responsibilities in a way that leaves us energized and satisfied at the same time.[4]

Several years ago, I did an informal survey with some of the women in our congregation, asking them what their passions were (other than the Lord or family). I received a lot of blank stares. After some prodding, a few women offered thoughts of what was meaningful to them—reading, art, knitting, etc.

Then, I asked how these activities brought them closer to God. One woman's eyes brightened—she was the knitter. Even I wondered, "How spiritual is that?"

She shared that she'd had several dreams where God told her to learn something new. She felt led to take up knitting. As she began knitting, she discovered that when her hands were busy, her mind focused. Normally, her mind was distracted when she prayed (don't we all struggle with that?), but when she knitted blankets and scarves for others as gifts, she was able to spend long stretches of time in intercession.

Her heart is knit together with the Lord.

My passions for writing and statistics are part of who I am, but there is another passion I have. Like my friend, God introduced a practical passion into my life a number of years ago. Also, like my friend, my busy mind sometimes makes it difficult for the Lord to connect with me.

Once my brain fully awakens, God's still small voice is drowned out in the steady stream of thoughts. I need extra help. I've noticed the Lord sometimes has to get my attention when my brain is mostly shut down. His practical passion for me is dreams. Others may get into the psychological symbolism of the images; I really don't. My interest is practical and best described in Job 33:14–18 (NKJV).

> For God may speak in one way, or in another, yet man does not perceive it. In a dream, in a vision of the night, when deep sleep falls upon men, while slumbering on their beds, then he opens the ears of men. And seals their instruction, in order to turn man from his deed, and conceal pride from man, he keeps back his soul from the Pit, and his life from perishing by the sword.

In other words, God sometimes has to use dreams because we just can't recognize a very important message any other way. This so applies to me.

One dream in particular stands out in my memory. God showed me that I had severely discouraged my daughter when she was growing up. Initially, I didn't realize that's what the dream was about. Over several months, the Lord interpreted the dream through a series of events, including introducing me to a young woman who was in the dream.

God could have just told me that I needed to repent for discouraging my daughter during her childhood. But I think he knew how devastated I would have been. He knows me, how I think, and what draws me closer to him, so instead he gave me a dream—a puzzle—and then helped me put it together. He wanted me to see the whole picture and not just show me my mistake. He brought a complete stranger to minister to me in a dream and then in real life. Fantastic. He revealed how wide his scope of work is in my life and the lives of my family. Miraculous.

What I love about exploring my dreams with the Lord is it's truly just him and me. It's our Secret Place—our place of trust, creativity, and wonder. In this place, we make eye contact.

How ironic. My best eye contact with the Lord is in my sleep.

Have we begun to pinpoint our passions? Are we ready to practically integrate them into our daily activities? Are we ready for any new directions that the Lord may be taking us?

This week, our last week (unless you're randomly working through the book), let's ask the Lord if there are things in our lives with which he wants us to energize the passions that he's placed in us and if there are any other areas where we're holding back from him. Are we ready to experience our Beloved in new ways?

Y'Didi (My Beloved), yes, I think I'm ready—and if I'm a little nervous, then please help me to be ready—to take our relationship to new levels. I understand that you know me from the inside out. You long to connect with me in ways that are unique to me. I want to relate to you in the way that you've created me. I want you to step into my life in ways that you've never done before. I'm ready, Lover of my Soul. In Yeshua's Name. Amen.

Let's take it to the Secret Place:

Have I pinpointed my passions? Please describe.

_____

_____

_____

_____

_____

_____

Have I thought of ways to integrate these passions into my everyday life? Describe.

_____

_____

_____

_____

_____

Write down some examples of how I can practically apply my passions this week.

_____

_____

_____

_____

_____

_____

End of Week Fifty-Two:

Did my Beloved interact with me in a new and unique way this week? If so, describe. Did this deepen our relationship? If so, how?

_____

_____

_____

_____

_____

_____

Conclusion

Making Eye Contact With God ~ and each other

It's hard to believe a year has passed!

Together, we've identified and (hopefully) overcome many of the barriers that kept us from making eye contact with God. We've also glimpsed more of God's heart and his longings.

Imagine, dear sisters, he loves us so much that he desires to connect deeply with us every day! He longs to surprise us with jewels of his affection.

My prayer is that this little devotional served as a springboard for our continued exploration of his passion. I trust that as we pursue this journey, we'll learn more about ourselves and the marvelously rich passions that God has planted in us. If you're like me, you may even need to reread portions—or all—of the book a few times to give the concepts a chance to seep into your spirit.

Toda raba (Thank you very much) for sharing this ride of faith and love with me.

May you soar with him. May you delight and give him pleasure. May you dance with him with all of your might. May you live your life in practical passion. May you make eye contact with God every day from now and into eternity.

✡ ✡ ✡

Please let me know if this devotional was meaningful to you. I would love to hear your stories of passion and how you and the Lover of your Soul connected. I'm also available to speak at your women's retreats or other special events.

Terri Gillespie
c/o Messianic Jewish
Publishers
6120 Day Long Lane
Clarksville, MD 21029

Or email me:
devotions@terrigillespie.com

Or visit my website:
www.terrigillespie.com

Notes

Chapter One
Week Five
1. LifeWay Biblical Solutions for Life, "Why They Flee: Study of Adults Who Switch Churches." (LifeWay Research, www.lifeway.com, October 27, 2006).
2. The Barna Group, "Born Again Christians Just as Likely to Divorce as Are Non-Christians." (www.barna.org, September 8, 2004). Accessed January 2008.
3. Stern, *Jewish New Testament Commentary*. (Clarksville: Jewish New Testament Publications, Inc., 1992), 204-205.

Chapter Three
Week Eleven
1. Wirt, *Billy: A Personal Look at Billy Graham*, the World's Best Evangelist (Wheaton: Crossways Books, 1997), 226.

Week Fifteen
2. Rogers and Hammerstein, "I'm Just a Girl Who Can't Say No," from the musical *Oklahoma*, (Opened on Broadway, 1943.) My sincere apologies to Mr. Rogers and Mr. Hammerstein for my edited version of their song.
3. *Nu* is a versatile Yiddish word that literally translates as "well", but depending on intonation it can mean all sorts of things. In this example it means: "Well, that's just the way it is."
4. Yiddish for explode.

Chapter Four
Week Seventeen
1. The Barna Group, "Goals and Priorities" (www.barna.org, Archived Topics, 2005). Accessed January 2008.

Chapter Five
Week Twenty-Four
1. By the way, I strongly recommend taking this sin to the *Lord* in the Secret Place. Do not confess to the person you are jealous of—unless they confront you first. The person you're envious of may not be

equipped to help you through this problem. This may cause unneces sary disharmony between you both, even after you overcome the sin.

Chapter Six
Week Twenty-Six
1. Brody, "PERSONAL HEALTH; A Second Opinion on Sunshine: It Can Be Good Medicine After All." (*The New York Times*, June 17, 2003). Archive accessed via www.nytimes.com.
2. The first night of Passover is when families participate in a delicious meal called a Seder using a Haggadah. For more information about Passover hosting your own Seder filled with symbolism of Yeshua/Jesus see *God's Appointed Times* by Barney Kasdan (Clarksville: Messianic Jewish Publishers, 1993), 25-38. See also the *Messianic Passover Haggadah* and *Messianic Passover Seder Preparation Guide*. All avail able through Messianic Jewish Resources Int'l., www.messianicjewish.net.

Week Twenty-Eight
3. The Roman rulers hired Jewish people to be their tax collectors. They were detested by the Jewish community for not only were they serving the enemy, but many overcharged their people and pocketed the money. Stern, *Jewish New Testament Commentary*. (Clarksville: Jewish New Testament Publications, Inc., 1992), 30.
4. Torah: the first five books of the bible. The Torah required that anyone who stole what was essential and showed no pity was required to pay back fourfold (Exodus 21:37(22:1)). Stern, *Jewish New Testament Commentary*. (Clarksville: Jewish New Testament Publications, Inc., 1992), 138.

Chapter Seven
Week Thirty-Three
1. Hyatt, *I'll Do It Myself* (Surrey, BC, Canada: Soaring Eagle Communication, 2007).

Week Thirty-Five
2. Chambers, *My Utmost for His Highest* Journal (Uhrichsville: Barbour Publishing, Inc., 1963), devotion for December 15th.

Chapter Eight
Week Thirty-Seven
1. Davidic worship is based on the worship established by King David. This praise and worship involves numerous musical instruments,

singing, Hebraic music, psalms, lifting up of hands, chanting, clapping of hands, processions and is also characterized by great joy. What is most unusual in modern Davidic worship and praise is dancing to the Lord. This is not dancing in a secular sense or dancing alone. Messianic dancing uses a strong Israeli-Hebraic style, and is done in unity with other worshipers.

Chapter Nine
Week Forty-One
1. *The Pursuit of Happyness*. Distributed by Columbia Pictures, 2006.

Chapter Ten
Week Forty-Six
1. On the first night of Hanukkah families light the Shamash (servant) candle then light the first of eight candles for the eight days of the Feast of Dedication. Some families also present loved ones with a gift each night. For more information about Hanukkah and how to celebrate this holiday in your own home see *God's Appointed Times* by Barney Kasdan (Clarksville: Messianic Jewish Publishers, 1993), 107-119. See also *Dedicate and Celebrate: A Messianic Jewish Guide to Hanukkah* by Barry and Steffi Rubin. These books are available through Messianic Jewish Resources Int'l., www.messianicjewish.net.

Week Fifty
2. *Chariots of Fire*. Released by Warner Brothers 1981.

Week Fifty-Two
3. Karen Scalf Linamen, *I'm Not Suffering from Insanity . . . I'm Enjoying Every Minute of It!* (Ada: Fleming H. Revell, 2002).
4. Ibid., 32.

Bibliography

Alexander, David and Pat Alexander. ed. *Eerdmans Handbook to the Bible*. Grand Rapids: William B. Eerdmans Publishing Company, 1983.

Arterburn, Stephen, Fred Stoeker and Mike Yorkey. *Everyman's Battle*. Colorado Springs: WaterBrook Press, 2000.

The Barna Group. "Born Again Christians Just as Likely to Divorce as Are Non-Christians." www.barna.org, September 8, 2004

_____. "Goals and Priorities." www.barna.org, 2005

Beck, William F, B.A., B.D., M.S.T., Th.D. *The Holy Bible: An American Translation*. New Haven, MO: Leader Publishing Company, 1976.

Blech, Rabbi Benjamin. *The Complete Idiot's Guide to Learning Yiddish*. Indianapolis: Alpha Books, 2000.

Brody, Jane E. "PERSONAL HEALTH: A Second Opinion on Sunshine: It Can Be Good Medicine After All." *The New York Times*, June 17, 2003.

Chambers, Oswald. *My Utmost for His Highest* Journal. Uhrichsville, OH: Barbour Publishing, Inc., 1963.

Collins, Brandlyn. *Getting Into Character*. New York: Wiley and Sons, Inc., 2002

Diamant, Anita. *The New Jewish Baby Book, 2nd Edition: Names, Ceremonies, Customs—A Guide for Today's Families*. Woodstock: Jewish Lights Publishing, 2005.

Hyatt, Glenda Watson. *I'll Do It Myself*. Surrey, BC, Canada: Soaring Eagle Communication, 2007.

Kasdan, Barney. *God's Appointed* Times. Clarksville: Messianic Jewish Publishers, 2007.

Lifeway Biblical Solutions for Life. "Why They Flee: Study of Adults Who Switch Churches." LifeWay Research, www.lifeway.com, October 27, 2006.

Linamen, Karen Scalf. *I'm Not Suffering from Insanity . . . I'm Enjoying Every Minute of It!* Ada: Fleming H. Revell, 2002.

Rosten, Leo. *The New Joys of Yiddish*. New York: Three Rivers Press, 2001.

ten Boom, Corrie. *The Hiding Place*. New York: Random House, Inc., 1982.

Silvious, Jan. *Big Girls Don't Whine*. Nashville: Thomas Nelson, Inc., 2003.

Stern, David H. *Jewish New Testament Commentary*. Clarksville: Jewish New Testament Publications, Inc., 1992.

Strong, James, LL.D., S.T.D. *The New Strong's Complete Dictionary of Bible Words*. Nashville: Thomas Nelson Publishers, 1996.

The Woman's Study Bible, Second Edition. (New Kings James Version) Nashville: Thomas Nelson. Inc., 2006.

Vander Meulen, Elizabeth L. and Barbara D. Malda. *His Names Are Wonderful: Getting to Know God Through His Hebrew Names*. Clarksville: Messianic Jewish Publications, 2005.

Wirt, Sherwood Eliot. Billy: *A Personal Look at Billy Graham, the World's Best Evangelist*. Wheaton: Crossways Books, 1997.

Movies:

Chariots of Fire. Released by Warner Brothers 1981.

End of the Spear. FoxFaith, 2005.

Independence Day. Distributed by Twentieth Century Fox, 1996.

The Pursuit of Happyness. Distributed by Columbia Pictures, 2006.

Acknowledgments

I read somewhere that the publishing of a writer's first book involves the encouragement, prayers, mentorship, and help of so many people that it takes pages and pages to thank everyone. If after you stalwart souls have read through the acknowledgments and I've forgotten anyone, please forgive me.

At the risk of this reading like a genealogical so-and-so begat so-and-so, here are my wonderful influencers:

Marlene, whom God used to call me back to writing; if she and Sharon hadn't walked through the doors of Congregation Beth Yeshua, who knows when I would have pursued learning the craft of my heart. Angie, the gold standard of writing; she continues to push me to be a better writer, and I'm honored to know her. My critique peeps—ACFW Crit1 and StoryCrafters—especially Cynthia and Julie, who took the time not only to give insightful evaluation, but to cheer me on to completion. Carrie, Kathy, and Wanda, your gentle exhortations meant so much. Thanks to my agent, Les, who challenges me to look into new territories.

Thanks to the Lederer editing staff, Rebecca and David. Thanks to Barry for believing in the vision.

To some of the women who have inspired me in powerful, unique, and amazing ways: my mother; my beautiful daughter, Rebekah ("Rivy"); my sisters; the two Debbies, the amazing wives of our amazing rabbis at Congregation Beth Yeshua. Also, Bobbi, Teresa, Hope, Susan, Kimberly, Pam, Cyn, Jules, Judy, Kathy, Margaret, Rhona, Marsha, Tina, Mindy, Melissa, Jennifer, Laurie, Arlene, and Molly. Special thanks to those who shared their stories with me to edify and teach. God bless you!

To the staff of the Messianic Jewish Alliance of America, thanks for your patience as I walked the halls like a zombie while still meeting deadlines. Most especially, thanks for the prayers.

To my husband, Bob—Thank you, honey, for your patience and not complaining when you didn't have clean underwear. You are an amazing man of God, and how grateful I am that he gave me a husband with whom I can laugh. I love you more today than I did yesterday.

To the King of my heart, you have amazed me with your loving kindness. When I think of where I should be but because of your love I'm not, I still get choked up. I love you and am eternally yours. Thank you for seeing me.

Other related resources from Messianic Jewish Publishers

Complete Jewish Bible
Presenting the Word of God as a unified Jewish book, here is an English translation for Jews and non-Jews alike. Names and key terms are presented in easy-to-understand transliterated Hebrew, enabling the reader to pronounce them the way Yeshua (Jesus) did!

His Names Are Wonderful
Getting to Know God Through His HEBREW Names
In Hebrew thought, names did more than identify people; they revealed their nature. God's identity is expressed not in one name, but in many. This book will help readers know God better as they uncover the truths in his Hebrew names.

God's Appointed Times
A Practical Guide for Understanding and Celebrating the Biblical Holidays
How can the biblical holy days such as Passover/Unleavened Bread and Tabernacles be observed? What do they mean for Christians today? Provides an easily understandable and hands-on approach. Discusses historical background, New Testament relevance, and prophetic significance.

The Voice of the Lord
Messianic Jewish Daily Devotional
Start your day with this unique resource. Twenty-two prominent Messianic contributors provide practical ways to apply biblical truth. The perfect companion to the *Complete Jewish Bible*.